Black and White Children in America: Key Facts

Children's Defense Fund

122 C Street, N.W.
Washington, D.C. 20001

(202) 628-8787
(800) 424-9602

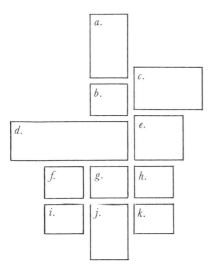

a. Steven Shames, b. Danny Lyon, Magnum, c. Steven Shames, d. Rick Reinhard, e. Steve Schapiro, Black Star, f. Mary Ellen Mark, Archive, g. Nathaniel K. Brooks, h. Steven Shames, i. Rick Reinhard, j. Bruce Davidson, Magnum, k. John David Arms, Geroboam.

The Children's Defense Fund gratefully acknowledges the support of the New York Times Company Foundation, Inc., in the publication of this book. We are also grateful to the Charles H. Revson Foundation, which provides funds for all CDF publications. The statements made and the views expressed, however, are solely the responsibility of the Children's Defense Fund.

Library of Congress number: 84-073490
ISBN 0-938008-39-0

Design by Stephen Kraft

Contents

FOREWORD

This report decribes the overall and comparative status of black and white children in America, the continuing inequality that plagues millions of black children, and the expensive waste in lives and dollars that results from our nation's failure to invest preventively in all our young—black and white, affluent and poor—alike.

Black Children are Sliding Backwards

Our principal conclusion is that black children are sliding backwards.

Compared to five years ago, black children are:

more likely to
- be born into poverty
- lack early prenatal care
- have an adolescent or single mother
- have an unemployed parent
- be unemployed themselves as teenagers
- not go to college after high school graduation

Compared to white children, black children are

twice as likely to
- die in the first year of life
- be born prematurely
- suffer low birthweight
- have mothers who received late or no prenatal care
- be born to a teenage or single-parent family
- see a parent die
- live in substandard housing
- be suspended from school or suffer corporal punishment
- be unemployed as teenagers
- have no parent employed
- live in institutions;

three times as likely to
- be poor
- have their mothers die in childbirth
- live with a parent who has separated
- live in a female-headed family
- be placed in an educable mentally retarded class
- be murdered between five and nine years of age
- be in foster care
- die of known child abuse;

four times as likely to
- live with neither parent and be supervised by a child welfare agency
- be murdered before one year of age or as a teenager
- be incarcerated between 15 and 19 years of age;

five times as likely to
- be dependent on welfare
- become pregnant as teenagers; and

twelve times as likely to • live with a parent who never married.

Poverty: The Great Child Killer

In 1985 affluent America, poverty is the greatest child killer. More American children die each year from poverty than from traffic fatalities and suicide combined. Twice as many children die from poverty than from cancer and heart disease combined.

Yet for the fifth consecutive year, in the face of the highest child poverty rate in 18 years, our national leaders have targeted poor children and families again for billions in new budget cuts. They seem to forget that poor children did not cause or choose their poverty. Nor can poor children escape poverty with governmental policies that snatch income, food, and health care from the poor in order to pay for defense increases and tax breaks for the wealthy.

Under the fiscal year 1986 Reagan administration budget, children would lose $5.2 billion. This is on top of $10 billion a year in cuts already made in survival programs for poor children and families since 1980.

At the same time, the administration proposed a $32 billion increase in defense spending in fiscal year 1986, on top of $178.3 billion in defense increases since 1980 to make American children more "secure" from external enemies.

By 1990, if current administration budget priorities succeed, every American will be spending 19 percent less on poor children and families and 86 percent more on the military.

American children need defense against the enemies within. Over a five-year period, more American children die from poverty than the total number of American battle deaths during the Vietnam War. Yet our national leaders dream about a multi-billion dollar "Star Wars" system to make our defenses impenetrable against enemy missiles. Why can't they dream of a smaller achievable war against child poverty—a war that saves and enhances rather than takes and threatens human life? Every poor American child could be lifted out of poverty in 1986 for less than half of the administration's proposed defense spending increase for that year alone.

American babies need defense against preventable infant mortality and birth defects. For two consecutive years, the decline in our national infant mortality rates—already a sad fifteenth in the world—has slowed. The national death rate for infants between one month and one year of age actually increased by 6 percent between 1983 and 1984. By 1990, 22,000 American babies will die primarily because of low birthweight. We can prevent at least one in eight of these infant deaths and thousands of handicapping conditions simply by providing their mothers prenatal care. Prenatal care saves lives as well as dollars. It costs $600 to provide a mother prenatal care. It costs about $1,000 a day to care for a premature baby in intensive care.

Tens of thousands of American preschool children need defense against preventable disease. While our nation plans to build 17,000 new nuclear weapons over this decade at an estimated cost of $71 billion, the administration budget only allows for a single month's stockpile of vaccination serum. Unless Congress adds to this request, two million fewer children will be immunized against DPT at a time when half of all black preschool children are not fully immunized against DPT and polio.

American children need to be protected against increasing child abuse. Every American supports a strong defense and well-defined national security goals. We certainly do. But don't children have a similar right to security against sexual and other abuse in day care centers and at home? An estimated 1.5 million children were reported abused and neglected in 1983, an increase of 200,000 children over the previous year. Why then are we cutting funding for programs designed to prevent and treat child abuse? One hour of our current military expenditure rate would pay for all federal child abuse prevention programs.

American children need defense against growing homelessness. A 1984 Department of Housing and Urban Development (HUD) study said that 22 percent of the homeless in shelters, not including runaway shelters, are children under age 18. Over 66,000 children are currently living without adequate, permanent shelter. Rather than seeking to provide decent housing and minimal income supports to help families weather unemployment and loss of shelter, our national leaders are emasculating low income housing programs and cutting millions more from the tattered survival net of Aid to Families with Dependent Children (AFDC). AFDC recipients, 66 percent of whom are children with an average daily benefit of $3.67, have been cut $1.7 billion since 1980.

American children need protection against too-early parenthood, which locks new generations of children and women into poverty. Recently released data from the Alan Guttmacher Institute show that the United States leads nearly all other developed nations of the world in rates of teenage pregnancy, abortion, and childbearing. The rates for white teenagers alone are twice as high as those of Canada, France, and England even though we have similar rates of sexual activity. And the maximum difference in birth rates occurs among girls under age 15, the most vulnerable teenagers.

The costs of adolescent parenthood are enormous—for the teen parents, for their children, and for society. Seventy-two percent of all white female-headed families with mothers 25 years of age and under and 85 percent of similar black families are poor.

In 1983, 525,000 babies were born to teen mothers, 10,000 to girls age 14 and under. Over 300,000 of these girls had not completed high school, and 36,000 had not completed ninth grade. About 31 percent of these births are paid for by Medicaid at an annual cost of $200 million. Sixty percent of all AFDC mothers had their first child as a teenager. Yet we are being told by some that we cannot afford $100 million this year to establish more comprehensive school-based clinics, which have demonstrated their effectiveness in reducing teen pregnancy rates. That's equivalent to one MX missile. Surely one less missile would not cripple our national security. Teenage parenthood will surely cripple the lives of thousands of children and their children.

Four Weasels That Hurt Children

Sojourner Truth, an illiterate slave woman, feminist, and anti-slavery fighter, had a knack for stating big truths simply. She said once: "I hear talking about the Constitution and the rights of man. I comes up and I takes hold of this Constitution. It looks mighty big, and I feels for my rights, but there aren't any there. Then I say, 'God, what ails this Constitution?' He says to me, 'Sojourner, there is a little weasel in it.'"

Well, there are some big weasels gnawing away at the constitutional and moral underpinnings of our democratic society that victimize millions of children. The first one is the *greedy military weasel* that can never seem to get enough. It currently spends $800 million a day, $33 million an hour, $555,000 a minute. Just a minute's worth of the military weasel meal would pay for the 14,000 monthly WIC food packages to feed pregnant women and infants that the administration cut in 1985.

Between now and 1990, this weasel will spend at least another $1.5 trillion—much more if the Reagan administration has its way. We must all curb this weasel before, in President Eisenhower's words, it "threatens to destroy from within what we are seeking to protect from without."

The second big weasel that threatens our democratic equilibrium and poor children is the *unfairness weasel* that must be ferreted out. Not only have poor children and families been made frontline casualties of the federal budget deficit reduction war, they have seen their federal taxes skyrocket while rich individuals and corporations reaped the biggest tax break in the nation's history in 1981.

The amount of federal tax paid by those with incomes below the federal poverty line increased 58 percent from 1980 to 1982 alone. In 1984, a working single mother with three children and a below-poverty income of $10,500 paid $1,186 in taxes, more than Boeing, General Electric, Dupont, Texaco, Mobil, and AT&T altogether paid in 1983, although these huge corporations earned $13.7 billion in profits.

What standard of fairness can justify this outcome in a democratic society?

The third weasel that hurts children is the *ignorance weasel*, which has created an enormous accuracy gap in public policy decision-making. Citizens have to dig hard to stay informed and to hold their leaders accountable. With great skill and sloganistic simplicity, our national leader has seized on a few kernels of truth about waste and abuse which infects some social programs, just as it infects some defense contractors, and tainted indiscriminately a whole harvest of fine programs that lifted millions of children and elderly citizens out of poverty in the 1960s and 1970s. Head Start works. It keeps children in school, at grade level, and out of costly special education. In the decade after Medicaid, black infant mortality rates decreased 50 percent. Economic growth alone, while important, would not have achieved these and other positive results.

Each of us must let our senators and representatives know what choices we want him or her to make for us and for our nation this year and every year.

The weak-will weasel. Our nation *can* eliminate child poverty and curb the teen pregnancy epidemic. Our individual and collective wills can achieve these goals. Our political leaders must stop turning our national plowshares into swords and bringing good news to the rich at the expense of the poor. But it will take strong and informed citizen action to redirect the perverted national spending priorities that permit so many American children to go hungry and die needlessly for lack of preventive health care. We must begin to translate the American Dream into daily individual and collective deeds that, over time, will change the portrait of continuing inequality drawn by the facts in this report.

What Can You Do?

One: Urge your Congressional delegation to make no new budget cuts in programs serving poor children and to restore successful preventive children's programs unfairly cut since 1980. Pay attention also to state and local budgets to ensure that children do not bear the brunt of budget cutbacks.

Two: Work for Congressional enactment of the provisions of the Children's Survival Bill included in Chapter Two. A national deficit reduction package which seeks to protect preventive children's programs of proven success, the Children's Survival Bill also provides for several modest demonstration programs designed to prevent teen pregnancy, school dropouts, and to build more self-sufficient youth. Tax relief for poor working families struggling to support their children is also a strong priority.

Three: Join our campaign to prevent adolescent pregnancy and to ensure poor mothers access to prenatal care. CDF's first priority is to prevent the first pregnancy. Our second priority is to ensure that teen mothers who have already had one child do not have a second child, as 22 percent now do within two years. The third priority is to make sure that pregnant teens receive adequate prenatal care so that prematurity, low birthweight, and birth defects are not added to their babies' already enormous burdens.

Teens constitute 14 percent of all births, but 20 percent of all low birthweight births. Low birthweight babies are 20 times more likely to die than babies born at normal birthweight. Proper prenatal care can help prevent low birthweight and reduce infant mortality. Yet only 47 percent of black teenage mothers and 58 percent of white teenage mothers get early prenatal care.

To help parents, communities, and policy makers combat teen pregnancy and ensure prenatal care for all mothers, CDF has prepared a series of materials including

- an *Adolescent Pregnancy Child Watch Manual*. Adolescent Pregnancy Child Watch seeks to help local communities learn more about adolescent pregnancy and develop effective action agendas for preventing children from having children.

- Currently, 60 Child Watch projects are in place in 28 states in collaboration with the National Council of Negro Women, the Association of Junior Leagues, the March of Dimes, and the National Coalition of 100 Black Women. We welcome your involvement. Please contact Julia Scott, Child Watch Coordinator.

- "Preventing Children Having Children", a summary of the adolescent pregnancy problem, is the first in a series of publications by CDF's Adolescent Pregnancy Prevention Clearinghouse. For more information, please contact Karen Pittman, Clearinghouse Coordinator.

- a *Comprehensive Prenatal Care Campaign Kit* contains state-by-state data on prenatal care, low birthweight births, teen births, and infant mortality. If you want to know how to launch a prenatal care campaign in your community, please write or call Dana Hughes, CDF's Prenatal Care Coordinator, at (800) 424-9602.

There are no single or easy answers to what is a very complicated phenomenon. Serious efforts to prevent adolescent pregnancy must be multi-strategic, comprehensive, and long-term; have clear, short-term and intermediate goals; and involve parents, citizens, leaders, and policy makers at all levels of government, the private sector, and the media.

Sex education and family planning are two pieces of the puzzle of adolescent pregnancy. Youth and adult jobs, job training, schooling, and the support services like child care that make them possible, are also critical pieces of the complex puzzle. Reversing the pervasive cultural messages that "anything goes" and sex is bliss without consequences often conveyed by TV, movies, rock music, and advertisements is another important piece. Finally, building self esteem, instilling hope, and sharing a vision of a future and sense of purpose with our young are critical if young people are to be motivated to delay too-early childbearing and to form healthy families.

How This Book is Organized

This book has two parts. Part One includes an overview of key facts and trends about black and white children and the Children's Survival Bill. Part Two includes the detailed tables on which Part One's conclusions rest. An appendix includes additional tables and a glossary.

Special thanks are owed Karen Pittman, Coordinator of CDF's Adolescent Pregnancy Prevention Clearinghouse; Janet Simons and Paul Smith of CDF's Research staff; Kay Johnson of CDF's Health staff; and Peggy Jarvis and Cindy Goodson of CDF's Public Affairs/Publications staff.

Marian Wright Edelman
President
Children's Defense Fund

PART 1

Births to Single Black Women, by State, 1980

State	Percentage	State	Percentage
Alabama	51.9%	Missouri	63.9%
Alaska*	22.8	Montana*/**	24.1
Arizona	47.4	Nebraska	57.2
Arkansas	57.0	Nevada**	48.5
California**	52.8	New Hampshire*	13.5
Colorado	40.3	New Jersey	60.6
Connecticut	62.6	New Mexico	25.4
Delaware	66.1	New York**	59.4
Dist. of Columbia	64.3	North Carolina	48.0
Florida	59.4	North Dakota*	11.0*
Georgia	52.0	Ohio**	60.2
Hawaii	11.4	Oklahoma	51.6
Idaho*	26.6	Oregon	50.7
Illinois	66.0	Pennsylvania	66.8
Indiana	58.5	Rhode Island	55.3
Iowa	55.5	South Carolina	47.2
Kansas	50.8	South Dakota*	16.5
Kentucky	57.5	Tennessee	58.2
Louisiana	50.3	Texas**	43.7
Maine*	21.0	Utah*	37.7
Maryland	58.2	Vermont*	32.1
Massachusetts	52.9	Virginia	52.5
Michigan**	52.7	Washington	40.8
Minnesota	54.2	West Virginia	52.0
Mississippi	52.3	Wisconsin	62.4
		Wyoming*	34.5
		U.S. Total	55.3

Source: National Center for Health Statistics, *Monthly Vital Statistics Report*, Vol. 31, No. 8, Supplement, Table 14, November 30, 1982, Washington, D.C.

* Fewer than 500 live black births in 1980.

**Mothers' marital status imputed from data on birth certificate.

Note: The statistic shown is an out-of-wedlock ratio. It increases if either the number of births to unmarried women increases *or* the number of births to married women falls.

Chapter One

OVERVIEW OF KEY FACTS AND TRENDS

Family Status

For the majority of white children, family means a mother and a father. This is not true for most black children.

- Eight out of every 10 white children live in two-parent families; only 4 out of 10 black children do.

- Thirty percent of black children under 3 live in households headed by someone other than their parents.

- The proportion of children living in female-headed families more than doubled between 1960 and 1984, from 9.0 percent to 19.7 percent. Today, 1 child in 5 lives in such a family. By 1990, 1 in 4 children will live in such a family.

- Black children are three and one-half times more likely than white children to live in female-headed households. Half of the black children in America live in female-headed households compared to one-fourth in 1960.

- The proportion of black children living only with their mothers increased from 41.9 percent to 51.1 percent between 1979 and 1983. Part of this rise was due to a decline in the number of two-parent families from 43.4 percent in 1979 to 40.7 percent in 1983. Most, however, was due to a drop in the number of children living in relatives' households without a parent present.

- One black child in 4 lives with a parent who has never married compared to 1 white child in 48.

- In 1982, over 55 percent of all births to black women were out of wedlock. Among black women under age 20 the proportion was over 86 percent. For 30 years, these out-of-wedlock ratios have increased inexorably. They have now reached levels that essentially guarantee the poverty of black children for the foreseeable future. In 1950, only about 18 percent of all black infants and 36 percent of black infants born to teenagers were out of wedlock. The driving fact in this trend has *not* been an increase in the number of black infants born to teenage mothers. Rather it has been a decline in the marriage rate among pregnant young black women.

- The proportion of black women who are mothers by the time they are age 20 has increased slightly since 1940, from 40 to 44 percent. What has changed dramatically is the frequency with which black teens marry. Since 1947, the marriage rate for pregnant 15 to 17 year olds has dropped about 80 percent. The rate for black 18 and 19 year olds is down about 60 percent.

Adolescent Pregnancy

- There were 523,000 births to teenagers in 1982; 146,000 or 27.9 percent were black and 69.2 percent were white. Teenagers account for 24.6 percent of all black births and 12.3 percent of all white births.

3

Percentage of Births to Women Under Age 20, 1982

■ Based on the percentage of all live births to women under age 20, the states and the District of Columbia can be ranked as follows.

States Ranked by Percentage of Births to Women Under Age 20

All Races			*Black/Nonwhite, 1982*		
Rank	*State*	*Percentage*	*Rank*	*State*	*Percentage*
1	Minnesota	8.9%	1	Hawaii	12.1%
2	Massachusetts	9.7	2	Utah	12.7
3	North Dakota	10.0	3	Colorado	13.2
4	New Hampshire	10.2	4	Oregon	14.6
4	Utah	10.2	5	Massachusetts	14.9
6	Nebraska	10.5	6	Washington	15.3
7	Connecticut	10.7	7	Alaska	16.1
7	Iowa	10.7	8	Minnesota	17.0
10	Alaska	10.9	9	New York	18.2
10	Hawaii	10.9	10	New Mexico	19.0
10	Vermont	10.9	11	West Virginia	19.1
10	Washington	10.9	12	Rhode Island	19.2
13	Wisconsin	11.0	13	Wyoming	20.0
14	New York	11.3	14	California	20.1
14	Rhode Island	11.3	14	North Dakota	20.1
16	Montana	11.4	16	Arizona	21.1
17	New Jersey	11.5	17	Iowa	21.4
18	Oregon	11.8	17	Kansas	21.4
19	Colorado	12.0	19	Virginia	21.7
19	South Dakota	12.0	20	Maryland	22.4
21	Idaho	12.1	21	Michigan	22.5
22	California	12.6	22	Washington, D.C.	22.8
23	Michigan	12.8	23	Ohio	23.1
23	Pennsylvania	12.8	24	Connecticut	23.2
25	Maine	13.1	25	Kentucky	23.8
26	Kansas	13.4	26	Nebraska	23.9
27	Virginia	13.8	27	Pennsylvania	24.5
27	Wyoming	13.8	28	New Jersey	24.6
29	Maryland	14.0	29	South Carolina	24.7
30	Ohio	14.2	30	Louisiana	24.9
31	Nevada	14.5	31	North Carolina	25.1
32	Missouri	14.9	32	Missouri	25.4
33	Indiana	15.2	32	Oklahoma	25.4
34	Arizona	15.6	34	Nevada	25.5
35	Illinois	16.2	34	Texas	25.5
36	Delaware	16.3	36	Alabama	25.6
37	Florida	16.4	37	Indiana	25.7
38	Texas	17.0	37	Florida	25.7
39	New Mexico	17.4	39	Tennessee	25.9
40	North Carolina	17.7	39	Wisconsin	25.9
41	Oklahoma	18.3	41	Georgia	26.6

42	West Virginia	18.4		42	Illinois	28.2
43	South Carolina	18.5		43	Mississippi	28.7
44	Louisiana	18.7		44	Arkansas	29.2
44	Tennessee	18.7		45	Delaware	29.8
46	Georgia	18.8				
47	Alabama	18.9				
48	Kentucky	19.5				
49	Washington, D.C.	19.7				
50	Arkansas	20.8				
51	Mississippi	21.9				

Source: State Vital Statistics Offices. Some data gaps filled with National Center for Health Statistics unpublished data. Rankings by Children's Defense Fund.

Note: States have the same averaged rank in cases where the percentages are the same. Rankings are based on percentages rounded to the nearest tenth of a point.

The following states have small numbers of births to nonwhite teens and are not ranked: Idaho, Maine, Montana, New Hampshire, South Dakota, and Vermont.

- In 1982, each month, nearly 3,000 girls ages 15 and younger gave birth. Almost 6 out of 10 of the births to teens under age 15 were to black teenagers.

- Births to unmarried teens occur 5 times more often among blacks than whites. However, birth rates for black teens, married and unmarried, have been *declining* while the birth rate among white unmarried teens has been *increasing* in recent years.

- The number of adolescent births has declined steadily since the early 1970s, when it peaked at over 650,000. One in 10 blacks 15 to 19 years old gave birth in 1982 compared to 1 in 7 in 1970. But this was more than twice the comparable white rate. However, the proportion of births to unmarried teens has been increasing. In 1950, 13.9 percent, in 1970, 30.5 percent, and in 1982, 51.5 percent of all adolescent births were out of wedlock.

- The upward trend in out-of-wedlock adolescent births parallels a general trend in the country. While the proportion of out-of-wedlock teen births has been growing, the proportion of births to unmarried adult women has been going up even faster. Teenagers gave birth to about 53 percent of all babies born outside marriage in 1973, but 38 percent in 1982.

- Only 54.1 percent of teens who gave birth at age 18 or 19 had completed high school compared to 84.4 percent who gave birth in their twenties. Among teenage mothers, 15 to 17 years old, less than 10 percent had completed high school in 1981.

- Nine states account for 50 percent of all births to teens (Calif., Tex., N.Y., Ill., Fla., Ohio, Pa., Mich., and Ga.). Nine states account for 50 percent of births to white teens (Calif., Tex., N.Y., Ohio, Pa., Ill., Fla., Mich., and Ga.). Eight states account for 50 percent of all births to black teens (N.Y., Tex., Ill., Fla., Calif., Ga., La. and N.C.).*

---

*These states are listed according to rank by size (i.e., number of births), rather than from rankings by percentages within states. This list includes the states with the largest number of births, usually the largest states.

Percentage of Births to Women Under Age 20 That Were Out of Wedlock, 1982

States Ranked by Percentage of Births to Women under Age 20 That Were Out of Wedlock

White, 1982

Rank	State	Percentage
1	Mississippi	19.2%
2	Alabama	20.1
3	Arkansas	23.4
4	Louisiana	23.5
4	Oklahoma	23.5
6	North Carolina	23.6
7	Texas	23.7
8	Georgia	24.2
9	South Carolina	24.5
10	Tennessee	25.2
11	Utah	26.4
12	Kentucky	27.6
13	Wyoming	27.9
14	Nevada	29.0
15	Idaho	29.2
16	Hawaii	30.7
17	Virginia	31.0
18	West Virginia	31.6
19	Kansas	31.9
20	Alaska	32.0
21	Florida	33.7
22	Missouri	34.3
23	North Dakota	35.0
24	Indiana	36.1
25	South Dakota	36.2
26	Michigan	37.0
27	Delaware	39.4
28	Ohio	40.0
29	Montana	40.4
30	New Mexico	41.4
31	Nebraska	41.7
32	Illinois	42.1
33	Iowa	42.2
34	Colorado	42.6
35	Pennsylvania	43.7
36	Washington	44.0
37	Maryland	44.3
38	Arizona	44.4
39	Oregon	46.0
40	California	46.5
41	Wisconsin	47.2

Black, 1982

Rank	State	Percentage
1	New Mexico	68.4%
2	Utah	72.0
3	Washington	73.4
4	Colorado	74.5
5	Texas	77.5
6	Oklahoma	81.0
7	California	82.3
8	Louisiana	82.9
9	Georgia	83.0
9	Kansas	83.0
11	South Carolina	83.4
12	Michigan	84.3
13	Nevada	85.5
14	West Virginia	85.7
15	Oregon	86.0
16	North Carolina	86.1
17	Arizona	86.3
18	Mississippi	86.5
19	Alabama	87.0
20	Kentucky	87.4
21	Virginia	87.8
22	Arkansas	88.3
23	Connecticut	88.7
24	Florida	88.8
25	Iowa	89.6
26	Delaware	90.2
27	Washington, D.C.	90.3
28	Tennessee	90.5
29	New York	90.8
30	Massachusetts	90.9
31	Indiana	91.4
31	Ohio	91.4
33	Minnesota	91.8
34	New Jersey	92.3
35	Rhode Island	92.4
36	Maryland	92.8
37	Wisconsin	93.1
38	Missouri	93.2
39	Nebraska	93.5
39	Pennsylvania	93.5
41	Illinois	93.6

42	Maine	47.4
43	Vermont	48.6
44	Rhode Island	49.6
45	Washington, D.C.	50.0
46	Minnesota	50.3
47	Connecticut	53.0
48	New Jersey	53.8
49	New York	56.2
50	Massachusetts	57.7
51	New Hampshire	59.2

Source: State Vital Statistics Offices. Some data gaps filled with National Center for Health Statistics unpublished data. Rankings by Children's Defense Fund.

Note: States have the same averaged rank in cases where the percentages are the same. Rankings are based on percentages rounded to the nearest tenth of a point.

The following states have small numbers of births to nonwhite teens and are not ranked: Alaska, Hawaii, Idaho, Maine, Montana, New Hampshire, North Dakota, South Dakota, Vermont, and Wyoming.

Children Without Homes

- Over 100,000 black children were in foster care in 1980. Almost one-third have been there for over 5 years.

- Almost 10 percent of America's black children are in families supervised by a child welfare agency, 4 times the supervision rate for white children.

- Black children are about twice as likely as white children to be living in institutions and are 4 times more likely to be living in correctional institutions.

Income and Poverty

- Regardless of family type, black families, earn significantly less than white families. The median family income of black families is less than 60 percent of that of white families. Half of all black families had incomes below $14,500 in 1983.

- Almost half of all black children are poor compared to 1 in 6 white children. Children make up 36.6 percent of the white population and 44 percent of the black population living in poverty.

- The gap between black and white family income has increased. The median black family income was 10 percent less in 1983 than it was in 1970, 5 times the decline among white families.

- Black children in female-headed families are the poorest in the nation. Half live in families with incomes below $6,100. Between 1977 and 1982, the median incomes of these children's families dropped 28.3 percent, far more than the declines suffered by any other group of children, black or white.

- Black children in two-parent families are twice as likely as white children in two-parent families to live below the poverty line. Black children in female-headed families are 3 times more likely to be poor than white children in such families.

■ Based on data comparing 1984 AFDC monthly payment levels to the monthly federal poverty level, the states and the District of Columbia can be ranked as follows.

States Ranked by Monthly AFDC Payments as a Percentage of the Monthly Federal Poverty Level, 1984

Rank	State	Percentage	Rank	State	Percentage
1	Alaska	91%	26	South Dakota	42%
2	California	73	27	Virginia	42
3	Connecticut	73	28	Maryland	42
4	Wisconsin	72	29	Wyoming	42
5	Vermont	70	30	Oklahoma	41
6	Minnesota	69	31	Idaho	41
7	New York	67	32	Ohio	40
8	Hawaii	64	33	Delaware	40
9	Washington	64	34	Indiana	37
10	Rhode Island	62	35	New Mexico	37
11	Michigan	57	36	Missouri	36
12	Massachusetts	52	37	Arizona	33
12	Oregon	52	38	Florida	32
14	North Dakota	51	39	Nevada	32
15	Maine	51	40	West Virginia	29
16	Montana	50	41	Georgia	28
17	Nebraska	49	42	Kentucky	28
18	Iowa	49	43	Louisiana	28
19	New Jersey	49	44	North Carolina	26
20	Pennsylvania	49	45	Arkansas	22
21	Kansas	48	46	Utah	21
22	Colorado	48	47	Texas	21
23	New Hampshire	46	48	South Carolina	20
24	Illinois	43	49	Tennessee	18
25	Washington, D.C.	43	50	Alabama	17
			51	Mississippi	14

Source: State Vital Statistics Offices. Some data gaps filled with National Center for Health Statistics unpublished data. Rankings by Children's Defense Fund.

Note: States with the same payment are assigned the same rank. Rankings are based on the actual dollar amount of the payment. Percentages shown are rounded to the nearest whole point.

- Whether black or white, young mothers under age 25 heading families are very likely to be poor. The poverty rates in 1983 were 85.2 percent for young black female-headed families and 72.1 percent for young white female-headed families. *But black female-headed families are much more likely to stay poor.* In female-headed families with older mothers ages 25 to 44, there is a 25 percentage points gap between black and white poverty rates.

Employment and Unemployment

- Only 67 percent of America's black children have an employed parent compared to 86 percent of white children. Black children are more than twice as likely as white children to have no parent employed and almost 4 times more likley to have no parent in the labor force.

- Between 1979 and 1984, there was a 3.6 percent drop in the proportion of black children with at least one employed parent, over 3 times the drop among white children.

- At all ages, black men and women are more likely to be unemployed than white men and women. In September 1984, about 15 percent of all blacks were unemployed compared to about 6 percent of all whites. Almost half the black teens looking for work were unable to find jobs.

- Black men and women at all educational levels are less likely to be employed than white men and women, and those who are employed earn less. The most striking differences are between white males and other workers. In 1982, the median income of white male college graduates was $29,000, black male graduates $19,000, white female graduates $18,000, and black female graduates $16,000.

- Black high school graduates are more than twice as likely to be unemployed as white high school graduates. Black male college graduates are unemployed at 3 times the rate of white male college graduates. The unemployment rate for young black college graduates jumped from 15.1 percent in 1978 to 23.9 percent in 1982—an increase of 58.3 percent. The unemployment rate for white college graduates rose about 51 percent from 5.7 percent to 8.6 percent.

- Young black college graduates have an unemployment rate almost as high as that of white high school dropouts. About 1 out of 4 young black college graduates cannot find jobs. Among black high school dropouts the picture is much worse, with more than half unemployed.

- Among female-headed families, young black women's cash incomes are 58.7 percent of all black women's; young white women's cash incomes are 39.7 percent of all white women's incomes. The difference reflects not the greater earning power of young black women, but the extremely low incomes of older black women. Almost two-thirds of black women age 25 and over who head families live below poverty.

- Blacks and women are over-represented in low-paying occupations and under-represented in high-paying occupations. Six out of 10 black men are in occupations with median weekly earnings below $300. Six out of 10 white men are in occupations with median weekly earnings above $300. Black women are 4 times more likely than white women to be in private household jobs paying an average of $131 a week.

- The unemployment rate among black teenagers is almost 3 times that of white teenagers. Only 2 out of 10 black teens currently holds jobs.

- Unemployment rates for all youths, black and white, rose markedly between 1978 and 1982, roughly doubling among high school graduates and those with some college education.

- Unemployment rates among young adults, 20 to 24 years old, are lower than those for teens, but black rates are still 3 times those of whites. Over one-fourth of the black 20 to 24 year olds who want jobs are unable to find them.

Maternal Employment and Child Care

- Black mothers play a crucial role in determining their families' incomes. Among children in families with annual incomes of $25,000 or more, more than 8 out of 10 black children under age 6 have working mothers compared to about half of comparable white children.

- Young black children in two-parent families are more likely than white children to have working mothers. Among young black children in female-headed families the reverse is true, although white children in these families are more likely to have mothers in the labor force.

- Black women enter or return to the labor force when their children are younger, and they are more likely to work full time. As a result, more black than white children need full-time day care at earlier ages. Four out of 5 employed black mothers with preschool children work full time compared to 3 out of 5 white mothers.

Child and Maternal Health

- Eight out of 10 white women but only 6 out of 10 black women receive prenatal care in the first three months of pregnancy.

- Nearly 1 in every 10 black women receives no or last trimester prenatal care. Among black teenage mothers under age 15, 2 in 10 receive no or last trimester care. Almost 60,000 babies are born annually to teen mothers who receive late or no prenatal care.

- The percentage of babies born to women who received late or no care increased slightly in all age groups, black and white, from 1981 to 1982. The most dramatic change was among very young black mothers under 15.

- Black babies are more than twice as likely as white babies to be low birthweight at birth (less than 5.5 pounds). Low birthweight infants are more than 20 times as likely to die in the first year of life. A pregnant women without prenatal care is 3 times as likely to have a low birthweight child. One in 8 black babies is underweight compared to 1 in 18 white babies.

- Babies born to teenage mothers are more likely to be underweight than those born to 20 to 39 year old mothers. Twenty percent of all low birthweight babies were born to teens.

- The infant mortality rate for blacks is about the same as the white rate twenty years ago. If the black infant mortality rate in 1982 had been as low as the white rate, 5,598 fewer black babies would have died.

- White children are more likely than black children to be immunized. Between 47 and 61 percent of black preschoolers are not fully immunized against one or more preventable diseases.

- Almost 40 percent of black children under age 17 had never visited a dentist in 1981. Half of all children under 17 had not seen a dentist in the last year, including two-thirds of the black children. Overall, white children average twice as many dental visits per year as black children.

- Between one-fifth and one-third of all black children and youth fall below the median white hemoglobin level, which is one indicator of poor nutritional status and anemia.

Vital Statistics Concerning Maternal and Infant Health for the United States, 1982

	Total	White	Nonwhite	Black
Infant Mortality Rate (infant deaths per 1,000 live births)	11.5	10.1	17.3	19.6
Number of infant deaths	42,401	29,659	12,742	11,642
Percentage of infants born at low birthweight (5.5 pounds or less)	6.8%	5.6%	11.2%	12.4%
Percentage of infants born at low birthweight to women under age 15	13.8	11.7	15.4	15.5
Percentage of infants born at low birthweight to women ages 15-19	9.3	7.6	13.2	13.7
Percentage of babies born to women who began prenatal care in the first 3 months of pregnancy	76.1	79.3	63.2	61.4
Percentage of babies born to women under age 20 who began prenatal care in the first 3 months of pregnancy	54.2	57.4	47.0	46.6
Percentage of babies born to women who received no prenatal care or none until the last 3 months of pregnancy	5.5	4.5	9.3	9.5
Percentage of babies born to women under age 20 who received no prenatal or none until the last 3 months of pregnancy	11.5	10.4	14.0	13.9
Percentage of all births to women under age 20	14.2	12.3	21.9	24.6

Source: National Center for Health Statistics, unpublished data.

Child Abuse and Death Rates

- Black infants are 3 times more likely than white infants to die of known child abuse. Black children are 3 to 4 times more likely than white children to be murdered.

- Black youth are more likely to die as a result of homocide while white youth are more likely to die as a result of suicide. White males are almost three times more likely than black males to commit suicide. Almost all the increase in teen suicides between 1973 and 1980 is concentrated among white males. The white female suicide rate increased slightly over this period, while the rate among blacks decreased.

Education

- Almost 2 black children out of 5 are growing up in a family whose head did not complete high school, twice the rate for white children. White children are almost 4 times more likely than black children to live in families headed by college graduates.

- Black children score fewer correct answers on reading tests than do white children; the older they get the worse they score. Black students at all ages are poorer readers than white students. However, significant reading and math gains were made by many black children during the 1970s, but the gap still remains. There is a 19 percentage point gap between the reading scores of black and white 17 year olds.

- Black students are twice as likely as white students to be suspended from school, to be corporally punished, or be out of school.

- Black students are far more likely than white students to be behind in school. Black 17 year olds are 3 times more likely than white 17 year olds to be 2 or more years behind the modal grade for their age. Almost half the black 17-year-old males are either behind in school or have dropped out. In 1982, about 1 black 18 to 21 year old out of 4 had dropped out of school. Forty percent of the black female dropouts give pregnancy as the reason for leaving school.

- Those black students who graduate from high school are now less likely than white students to attend college. Although college attendance rates were about the same for blacks and whites in 1977, by 1982 whites were about 45 percent more likely than blacks to attend college. Poverty appears to be the key to low college attendance rate among blacks: 18.8 percent of poor black high school graudates and 34 percent of black graduates above poverty attended college in 1983.

Chapter Two

A Children's Survival Bill

A Positive Agenda for Children

The Children's Survival Bill is a legislative agenda for children, adolescents, and families for the Ninety-ninth Congress. It is an agenda of governmental investment for human survival and opportunity as well as for budgetary prudence and strength. The Bill is based on a sound and simple premise: an investment of scarce resources in our nation's children will protect our nation's future.

Children are the country's future workers and taxpayers, its future leaders, artists, teachers, and scientists. Today's children must shoulder tomorrow's national debt, finance its Social Security system, and lead this country into the twenty-first century. All Americans have a stake in making healthy and educated children into self-sufficient, creative, and productive adults.

Wise investment in children now is sound economic policy in a time of fiscal restraint. Research proves that children's programs that provide services like prenatal care and immunization save us more money than we spend on them. It costs about ten dollars to provide a baby with a series of immunizations, compared to hundreds of thousands of dollars for a lifetime of care for a child with severe disabilities caused by preventable sickness. Every dollar spent on comprehensive prenatal care saves two dollars in health care in the first year of an infant's life alone.

Second, investment in children is an intergenerational compact which protects our future security. Children need help during the eighteen years it takes them to reach adulthood. But today's adults will later turn to these children for support during retirement years. In the future, there will be more elderly people for the nation's economy to support. To protect ourselves in our old age, we must see to it that today's and tomorrow's children grow into productive and compassionate adults, because the security of all of us will come to rest on their shoulders.

But the children of the 1980s are an endangered group. Children are the poorest age group in America. The child poverty rate is at its highest level in twenty years. More than one in five children in this country live in poverty. One in four preschoolers is poor. Black and white, Hispanic and Asian, millions of children are now suffering the range of problems caused by poverty.

Too many children live in single-parent households. If that parent is a mother under the age of 25, this is almost a guarantee of a lifetime in poverty. These children are four times more likely to be poor than those in two-parent families. In 1983, 73.8 percent of young single-parent white families and 84.8 percent of young single-parent black families were poor.

Child poverty is also growing because teenage mothers are having children at a rate of half a million a year, and over 50 percent of these young women are single, thus adding another turn to the cycle of poverty. Adolescent pregnancy poses a complex problem for all communities— black, white and Hispanic.

Many children in traditional two-parent families are poor because their parents are unemployed—still. Despite our economic recovery, there are 5.4 million children with at least one parent unemployed and another 5.4 million children with no parent in the labor force.

But poverty is only one strike against our children's future and that of our nation. Our children are not as healthy as they should be. America ranks seventeenth in the world in keeping infants alive during their first year of life—behind many other industrialized nations. One in three children in America has never seen a dentist.

More children are reported abused each year in state after state. Families are falling apart, forcing children into the already overloaded foster care system.

Millions of children are left alone during the day while parents work at low-paying jobs because decent child care is either unavailable or unaffordable.

Too few adolescents are acquiring adequate skills for gainful employment. As a result, they are missing the opportunity to contribute to themselves or to their country's health and prosperity.

In these times of tight budgetary limits, society cannot afford to pay the high costs of waste and neglect. For example, it costs
• over $12,000 a year to house an inmate in a state prison, and
• over $16,000 a year for institutional care for a foster child.

Society cannot afford these high costs in the best of times, and the federal government most assuredly cannot afford them in the face of the largest budget deficit in history. Shortsighted policies by the Reagan administration that create crises among the young must be rejected as swiftly and firmly as shortsighted policies that create crises in our national budget and economy. The budget cuts in 1981, many of them at the expense of programs for children, were followed by a sharp rise in child poverty, by increasing reports of child abuse, hunger, sickness, and despair. Recognizing these results, Congress soundly rejected the additional Reagan administration proposals for budget cuts in children's programs in 1983 and 1984 and must do the same in 1985.

Just as prudent and economically sound steps must be taken to deal with the deficit crisis, so must proven, cost-effective steps be taken to rescue children from the crises they face. It is time to invest in our youth before they become ill, are left alone, have a baby, or drop out of school.

The Children's Survival Bill is an important first step toward these goals. It is a sound and balanced deficit reduction package. The Bill invests additional federal resources—about $14 billion—in cost-effective programs known to prevent child abuse and neglect, infant mortality and ill-health, malnutrition, illiteracy, teen pregnancy, despair, and dependency. The Bill proposes to offset these costs and yield a net of more than $25 billion in deficit reduction by eliminating tax loopholes now sheltering wealthy corporations and individuals, by imposing taxes on luxury items, and by eliminating funding for the controversial MX nuclear missile. There are, of course, a number of additional tax and military proposals that could be substituted to generate comparable savings.

The first Children's Survival Bill was developed for the Ninety-eighth Congress. Introduced by Senator Christopher Dodd (D-Conn.) and Representative Geraldine Ferraro (D-N.Y.), along with close to 100 congressional cosponsors from both par-

ties, the Bill served as a focal point for national concern about the plight of our nation's children. It proposed modest funding restorations in many of the programs for children and families severely cut back in 1981 and 1982. Many of these proposals were then adopted by Congress. After a total of $10 billion had been cut from programs for children and families in 1981 and 1982, more than $1 billion was added back in 1983 and another $1 billion in 1984. This is a start, but we have a long way to go to repair the damage and reach out to move more children out of poverty.

This year's bill calls for funds to be invested in sound, proven current programs for children like

• Head Start—a motivating program for young children that has a fifteen-year track record of success. For every one dollar invested in Head Start, three dollars are returned in reduced public expenditures and increased public receipts. Head Start children are less likely to end up pregnant as teens or on welfare, and more likely to enter vocational school, college, or the workforce.

• WIC—the Women, Infants, and Children feeding program, which study after study has found a success. A $35-a-month WIC nutritional package for an infant can save far more than the $1,400 a week it costs to hospitalize an infant for treatment of malnutrition.

• Chapter 1—the Education of the Disadvantaged program has a history of teaching young children to read and compute at a cost of approximately $625 per year compared to the more than $3,000 cost of keeping a child back to repeat a grade. Currently, nearly 10 million children repeat at least one grade during the course of their education.

• Maternal and child health programs—programs which are especially cost effective. Every dollar spent on comprehensive prenatal care saves two dollars in the first year of an infant's life alone because of reduced need for hospital care.

The Bill also proposes modest investments in creative new endeavors similarly premised on prevention: a drop-out prevention program to explore successful approaches to keeping adolescents—especially teenage mothers—in school; small grants to encourage states to improve the monitoring and supervision of child care facilities in order to improve the quality of care and prevent abuse or neglect of children; and incentives to maximize child care resources by greater cooperation with elementary and secondary schools.

This year, the Children's Survival Bill will also address the alarming problem of children having children—adolescent pregnancy. This complicated problem requires multiple strategies. First, we must prevent the first pregnancy, and then we must ensure that teens who have already had one child do not have a second. It is also critical to make sure that teenage mothers receive adequate prenatal care so that prematurity, low birthweight, or birth defects are not added to their babies' already stacked decks. Such elements as health and family planning efforts, job training and youth employment, schooling and child care are woven throughout the new Children's Survival Bill. The Bill also places priority on important demonstration projects, such as school-based comprehensive service centers, with proven records of success in preventing adolescent pregnancy.

The Children's Survival Bill also addresses another major national problem facing families: the unfair tax burden on the poor. Currently, federal taxes for families in poverty are going up, while they are declining for all other income groups. In the context of the current national discussion of tax reform, this year's Children's Survival Bill sets forth a number of proposals designed to establish tax fairness.

A section-by-section summary of the new Children's Survival Bill follows. Title I, "Essential Preventive Programs for Children," makes positive investment in children, adolescents, and their families:

• Section 1 helps keep families together through investments in federal programs for troubled children and families.

• Section 2 provides low-income families with affordable, quality child care so that children are not left alone or under inadequate care while their parents work or go to school.

• Section 3 ensures mothers and children access to prenatal care and health services in order to prevent infant mortality, birth defects, and costly childhood sickness and disease.

• Section 4 helps children and adolescents gain the education and skills they need for self-sufficiency in adulthood.

• Section 5 provides children and families with more adequate food and nutrition.

• Section 6 assists children and families most in need with a minimal level of support and opportunity for self-sufficiency.

• Section 7 brings tax fairness to working families in poverty, especially large and single-parent families.

• Section 8 helps adolescents and young adults gain job training and employment at wages that allow for self-sufficiency.

Title II of the Children's Survival Bill, "Reform and Elimination of Tax Subsidies and Weapons Systems," includes a range of proposals, many of which were endorsed by the U.S. Department of Treasury in its tax simplification plan, designed to produce additional federal revenue for investment in children and for deficit reduction.

This new Children's Survival Bill will be introduced in Congress and referred to many different committees. Because the Survival Bill is an omnibus piece of legislation, much like the Economic Equity Act for Women, Congress will not consider it in its entirety. There will never be a single vote on the Children's Survival

Bill. Its many separate proposals will, however, be considered by the Ninety-ninth Congress initially as it develops a budget for the 1986 fiscal year, and later when it moves to implement that budget. Support for the Children's Survival Bill means support for positive investment in children.

For more information, contact Mary Bourdette or the following CDF staff members on particular sections: Title I: Section 1, Marylee Allen; Section 2, Helen Blank; Section 3, Sara Rosenbaum; Section 4, Noe Medina; Section 5, Helen Blank; Section 6, Marylee Allen; Section 7, Mary Bourdette or Jim Weill; Section 8, Karen Pittman. Title II: Paul Smith.

Section-by-Section Summary

Title I: Essential Preventive Programs for Children

SECTION 1: TROUBLED CHILDREN AND FAMILIES:

Child abuse, neglect, emotional disturbance, running away, and many other special problems of children are often associated with troubled families. Services known to prevent and treat these problems of children and adolescents are available for only a fraction of the children in need. The proposals in this section seek to build upon successful federal programs for children with special needs.

(a) Child Abuse and Family Violence: Assists the more than 1.5 million children reported as victims of abuse and neglect by appropriating $41.5 million (an increase of $15.5 million) for the Child Abuse Prevention and Treatment Program. In addition, it provides shelter and related services to victims of family violence and their children by initially appropriating $26 million for the recently enacted Family Violence Prevention and Services Program.

(b) Child Welfare Services: Strengthens services for abused and neglected

children by appropriating $266 million (an increase of $66 million) for the Title IV-B Child Welfare Services Program and by extending state authority to utilize unused foster care funds for services for children at risk of placement or in care.

(c) Social Services Title XX: Helps troubled families with children through crisis assistance, child care, and special support services by providing $3.65 billion (an increase of $950 million) for the Social Services Block Grant (Title XX) so that all states, particularly the 45 which have experienced increased reports of child abuse and neglect, may respond with appropriate protective services. States would be required to match federal funds at a 75/25 rate and the increased service funds would be equally divided between child care and other social services.

(d) Foster Care: Extends support and protections to children in the federal foster care program, especially older adolescents up to age 21 who are still in school or training, and those in supervised independent living programs, and makes permanent the protections for those placed in foster care voluntarily by their parents.

(e) Runaway and Homeless Youth: Helps the approximately 1.5 million children who are runaway or homeless by appropriating $50 million (an increase of $26.7 million) for the Runaway and Homeless Youth Program. Currently less than 20 percent of these youngsters are served by federally funded shelters.

(f) Juvenile Justice and Delinquency Prevention: Assists states to meet the needs of youth in the juvenile justice system by appropriating $100 million (an increase of $30 million) for the Juvenile Justice and Delinquency Prevention Program.

(g) Child and Adolescent Mental Health: Helps seriously emotionally disturbed children and adolescents whose needs often fall through bureaucratic cracks by encouraging states to improve coordination among the child welfare, juvenile justice,

15

mental health and special education systems. Appropriates $7 million (an increase of $3.1 million) specifically for the Child and Adolescent Service System Program, funded as part of the adult Community Support Program.

SECTION 2: CHILD CARE:

Child care is essential if women are to work to support their families, and if children are to receive supervision and care. Yet a national crisis has developed as the supply of decent, affordable child care lags far behind the demand, so much so that as many as 6 to 7 million children may be left alone while their parents work, and many women must depend on welfare simply because affordable child care is unavailable. This section contains a number of creative approaches for expanding the availability of child care affordable to low income parents, and for improving the quality of care for children.

(a) Expand Child Care Availability: The following proposals offer a range of options to expand the availability of child care for low income families.

(1) Head Start: Provides approximately 60,000 additional children with a Head Start opportunity by appropriating $1.22 billion (an increase of $146 million). Currently Head Start serves only 18 percent of eligible children.

(2) Social Services Title XX: Ensures child care for approximately 200,000 additional low income children by providing $3.65 billion (an increase of $950 million) for the Social Services Block Grant, Title XX. Requires states to match federal funds at a 75/25 ratio, and reserves half the increased services funds for child care.

(3) Dependent Care Tax Credit: See Section 7(d).

(4) Child Care in Schools: Assists schools in providing child care and early childhood education for four and five year olds by appropriating $50 million for a competitive grant demonstration program with prefer-

ence to schools serving low income children under a new Chapter III of the Education Consolidation and Improvement Act. Requires state or local matching funds and sliding fee scales, age-appropriate curricula, appropriate state or federal standards, parent involvement and staff experienced with young children.

(5) Child Care for Adolescent Mothers: Helps teen mothers finish high school, by providing comprehensive services, including child care, through two new demonstration programs: the Dropout Prevention and Recovery Program funded at $58.5 million, and School Based Child Care funded at $50 million. See Section 4(c)(1) and (2).

(6) Child Care for Disadvantaged College Students: See Section 4(d)(1-3).

(7) Child Care in Public Housing: Helps public housing agencies provide child care by targeting $15 million for contracts with community based nonprofit child care agencies.

(8) Child Care Expenses for AFDC Recipients: Helps enable AFDC recipients to work by altering the order of the eligibility computation so that child care costs are disregarded last when calculating AFDC eligibility and benefits at a cost of $25 million. This will eliminate the current inequity between working AFDC recipients who receive subsidized child care and those who rely on the AFDC child care disregard for their child care expenses.

(b) Improve Child Care: The following provisions will improve the quality of child care services, a need highlighted by reports of abuses in day care centers.

(1) Standards: Improves and increases licensing and monitoring of child care services by providing states with $50 million in incentive grants to bring federally funded child care into compliance with, at a minimum, the Health, Education, and Welfare Day Care Requirement of 1980.

(2) Training: Improves training of

child care and other human service workers by allocating $100 million of the Title XX increase for this purpose, with a requirement that $10 million be directed to community based nonprofit agencies for support of family day care homes. See Section 2(a)(2).

(3) Child Development Associate Scholarships: Further improves the quality of child care staff by providing $1.5 million, divided among the states, to support scholarships for individuals seeking a Child Development Associate credential.

(4) Child Care Food: See Section 5(a).

(c) Maximize Child Care Resources: These provisions will maximize child care resources and help families locate services.

(1) School Age Programs/Resource and Referral: Helps families locate appropriate child care and expands community child care resources by providing $20 million for start up costs for resource and referral centers and for school age child care programs.

(2) Loan and Grant Program: Provides $20 million for child care start-up costs and renovation and equipment costs, including costs for equipment for the Child Care Food Program.

SECTION 3—HEALTH:

Basic medical care is necessary for survival and development, and is also cost effective. Yet thousands of pregnant women and children are not receiving the prenatal and preventive health services known to reduce infant mortality, birth defects, childhood diseases, and other costly complications of neglect. The following proposals build upon effective federal health programs so that lives and dollars can be saved.

(a) Maternal and Child Health Block Grant: Ensures basic prenatal care, checkups, immunizations and other essential health services to additional

low-income mothers and children by providing $529 million (an increase of $51 million) to the Maternal and Child Health Block Grant.

(b) Community Health Centers: Provides comprehensive health services to low income families through the Community Health Centers program. Studies show that comprehensive health clinics deliver high quality care that can reduce hospitalization rates between 25 and 40 percent. Provides $425 million (an increase of $26 million) by reauthorizing the program and repealing the Primary Care Block Grant Program.

(c) Family Planning: Provides essential, cost-effective health, family planning and education services to over 1 million young women and mothers by reauthorizing the program for three years and appropriating $185 million (an increase of $42.5 million) for family planning services for FY 1986. Studies show this program yields savings of $1.80 for every $1.00 invested.

(d) Immunization: Ensures all children age-appropriate immunizations against polio, diphtheria, measles, tetanus, whooping cough, and mumps by providing sufficient federal funding for this effort. Over 2 million *fewer* children are now receiving immunizations than in 1981; less than half of black preschool children are immunized against diphtheria-tetanus-pertussis and only 39 percent against polio. A Centers for Disease Control study indicates for every dollar spent on measles vaccinations, about $10 was saved in medical care and long-term care by reducing deafness, retardation, and other problems.

(e) Migrant Health Centers: Assures additional migrant families basic health care by providing $55 million (an increase of $5.7 million) for migrant health centers.

(f) Medicaid: Medicaid is the most important public health program in this country, and yet it reaches fewer than half of all poor children and

their families. The following proposals seek to improve the Medicaid program to ensure preventive health and other medical services especially critical to pregnant women and poor children.

(1) Pregnant Women and Children: Extends medical assistance over a two-year phase-in period to all pregnant women and children living below the federal poverty level. Coverage would be extended to children under six and all pregnant women in FY 1986 at a cost of $800 million, with coverage extended to children under 18 in FY 1987.

(2) Prenatal Services: Requires states to provide pregnant women with all medically necessary prenatal delivery, and postpartum services, regardless of whether such services are provided to the general Medicaid population, and without "amount, duration, or scope" limitations on coverage of such services other than medical necessity. Includes outreach and health education activities. Women who receive no prenatal care are three times more likely to have low birthweight babies, whereas every dollar spent on comprehensive prenatal care saves $2 in the first year alone of infant life. The estimated cost for increased care is $137.5 million.

(3) Pregnant Adolescents: Avoids the denial of Medicaid coverage to pregnant adolescents whose parents do not or cannot provide them with adequate medical care by prohibiting states from deeming income from parents to minor pregnant adolescents. Teen mothers account for one-fourth of low birthweight babies—a tragic and costly risk that can be significantly reduced by prenatal care.

(4) Medically Needy Pregnant Women and Children: Improves coordination of health services for poor women and children by requiring states to treat, as an incurred medical expense, the cost of services furnished to medically needy pregnant women and children by public clinics funded under Title V of the Social Security Act, or other federal public health programs, so

that they may qualify for Medicaid coverage. This would cost approximately $200 million.

(g) Supplemental Food (Women, Infants, and Children): Ensures supplemental food to approximately 3.4 million low-income children and pregnant women at nutritional risk—about 40 percent of those eligible—by providing $1.7 billion (an increase of $200 million) for the highly successful WIC program. Provision would also reauthorize the WIC program for three years at gradually increasing levels.

SECTION 4: EDUCATION:

An adequate and effective education is necessary for the development of skilled, trained, and productive young adults who will contribute to the nation. This section contains a range of education proposals designed to help children, including those with special needs, adolescents at risk of pregnancy, and those who are adolescent parents, attain self-sufficiency. The proposals include federal programs with long track records of success, and promising new demonstration efforts aimed at preventing pregnancy and other factors that cause youth to drop out of school.

(a) Successful Federal Programs: The following proposals expand existing cost-effective federal education programs.

(1) Education of Disadvantaged Children: Provides an additional 400,000 educationally disadvantaged children with the effective services of Chapter I of the Education Consolidation and Improvement Act, by appropriating $4.1 billion (an increase of $400 million).

(2) Bilingual Education: Provides an additional 55,000 students with bilingual education services, by appropriating $230 million (an increase of $91 million).

(3) Desegregation Assistance: Improves and expands the Magnet

Schools Assistance Act by providing $150 million (an increase of $75 million).

(4) Handicapped Education: Assists school districts in providing appropriate education for handicapped children by providing $1.33 billion (an increase of $220 million) and supporting all 94-142 programs at the fully authorized funding levels.

(b) Early Childhood: The following proposals represent modest investments in the early education of at-risk children.

(1) School-Based Early Childhood Education: See Section 2(a)(4).

(2) Early Childhood Education Incentive Grants: Encourages school districts to provide supplemental educational services for educationally disadvantaged four and five year olds by providing $100 million in grants under Chapter I of the Education Consolidation and Improvement Act.

(c) Adolescents: The following propose small investments in creative new school-based efforts to prevent adolescent pregnancy and school dropouts, and to encourage troubled adolescents to return to school.

(1) Dropout Prevention and Recovery Act: Addresses the problem of school dropouts by providing $58.5 million for a new effort to gather uniform, nationwide information, and to develop and fund demonstration projects aimed at keeping potential dropouts in school, and returning others back to school.

(2) School-Based Comprehensive Service Centers: Offers a range of services like health, counseling, and child care that meet the special needs of students, including those at risk of pregnancy, pregnant adolescents, teen parents, and potential dropouts, by providing $100 million for school-based comprehensive service centers. One successful 10-year program reduced the fertility rate for the school female population dramatically, and ensured that 87 percent of pregnant students graduated from high school.

(3) School-Based Student Enterprises: Broadens students' vocational experiences and improves academic skills by providing $10-million for school-based student enterprise projects.

(4) Effective Schools Development Act: Encourages and supports creative school-based projects of demonstrated success to improve the education offered to students by providing $100 million.

(5) University-High School Partnerships: Improves preparation of disadvantaged students for post-secondary education or employment through partnerships among universities, high schools, community-based organizations, and businesses and funded at $25 million.

(d) Higher Education: The following changes in the Higher Education Act increase the availability of child care for low-income college students.

(1) Child Care Services: Makes child care services available to low-income first generation college students by providing $15 million for this purpose.

(2) Child Care Work Experience Programs: Increases the availability of child care services by providing $10 million for work experience in this area.

(3) College-Based Child Care: Expands the supply of child care facilities by providing $50 million for construction, reconstruction, and renovation of facilities on college campuses.

SECTION 5: CHILD NUTRITION AND FOOD STAMPS:

All children need adequate nutrition to grow up healthy and without developmental problems. Yet every night, too many of America's children go to bed hungry. This section improves and expands existing food programs to provide children and families nutritional assistance. Several of the provisions were recommended by the Presidential Task Force on Food Assistance.

(a) School Food and Other Child Nutrition Programs: Provides more adequate food and nutrition for children by improving eligibility and reimbursement levels for the School Lunch, School Breakfast, and Child Care Food programs. Reauthorizes the Summer Food, Nutrition, Education, and Training—Section XIV—of the National School Lunch Program and the State Administrative Expense Program with technical changes. The improvements would cost approximately $220 million.

(b) Food Stamps—Benefit Levels Adjustment: Ensures needy families food assistance benefits based on the projected average costs of the Thrifty Food Plan for each fiscal year. The Thrifty Food Plan is the minimal food plan devised by the U.S. Department of Agriculture, but benefits fall below the cost of the Plan due to unnecessary time lags in benefit adjustment. This provision will assure more adequate food assistance at a cost of $500 million to $600 million.

(c) Food Stamps—Work Related Expenses: Restores from 18 percent to 20 percent the proportion of wages that a working poor family can allocate to work-related expenses and taxes. Since 1981, when the deduction was lowered, 1.3 million working families have lost all or some of their food stamps. The estimated cost is $50 million.

(d) Food Stamps—State Option for Monthly Reporting and Retrospective Accounting: Converts these burdensome and costly federal mandatory procedures into a state option, and requires those states that elect retrospective accounting to provide supplemental benefits for families that experience a sudden, significant loss of income and would be harmed by the state's accounting method, at an estimated cost of $0 to $25 million.

(e) Food Stamps—Asset Limit Adjustment: Assists needy families, especially unemployed families, by raising the asset limit (both overall and for cars) to partially reflect the increased cost of living since 1971 when the current limit was set. This

provision was recommended by the President's Task Force on Food Assistance and costs about $200 million.

(f) Food Stamps—Child Care Deduction: Assists low-income working mothers with child care expenses by restoring the separate child care deduction. This provision would cost about $15 million.

(g) Food Stamps—Shelter Cost Adjustment: Assists needy families with very high shelter costs by raising the maximum shelter deduction from $134 to $155. This is especially important for families whose heating bills have soared in recent years, forcing them to choose between heating and food for their families. The provision would cost about $75 million.

(h) Food Stamps—Reinstate Outreach Program: Informs eligible families of the rules, requirements, and application procedures for food stamps by reinstating the outreach component abolished in 1981. Many of the neediest families remain outside the Food Stamp Program because they do not understand eligibility requirements. The cost of this provision is $5 million to $10 million.

(i) Food Stamps—Modify Residency Requirement: Assures homeless persons food stamps by modifying current residency requirements. Currently, some of the most destitute people are denied food stamps because they have no "residence." This provision was recommended by the President's Task Force on Food Assistance, and the costs are negligible.

(j) Food Stamps—Child Support Disregard: Helps needy families by extending the $50 AFDC Child Support disregard to food stamps. This provision, which facilitates uniform program administration, also encourages more effective child support enforcement. The estimated cost is $50 million.

SECTION 6: FAMILY SUPPORT:

AFDC—Aid to Families with Dependent Children—is the program of last resort for millions of women and children in poverty. It is a frayed lifeline, however, barely providing for necessities, and serving less than half the families in poverty. This section proposes to increase the support available to those most in need and to assist families to become more self-sufficient.

(a) Increase Support for Needy Families: The average support for each child on AFDC is $3.67 per day. This is a meager amount that must cover all shelter, clothing, and other necessities, and is an amount that has actually decreased in value in recent years. The following provisions propose a gradual step-by-step movement toward a minimum national benefit level for AFDC families.

(1) State Incentives to Increase Benefits: Helps families in need by encouraging states to maintain the purchasing power of AFDC benefits against inflation by offering a higher federal matching rate to states that increase benefits. This would reward states that have increased benefits and encourage other states to do so at a cost of approximately $300 million.

(2) State Standards of Need Adjustment: Requires states, by October 1, 1988, to adjust their state needs standards to fully reflect changes in living costs over the last 20 years. The standard is a state figure that purports to represent, but rarely does, the amount of money families need for reasonable subsistence. It is used for various AFDC eligibility computations. Congress last required an adjustment in 1969, and few states have since adjusted their standard commensurate with inflation.

(3) National Minimum Benefit: Helps children in eligible poor families by ensuring them, effective October 1, 1989, support—AFDC and Food Stamps—at least equal to 75 percent of the federal poverty level. States would then be encouraged to continue to raise benefits. The minimum benefit would increase AFDC levels for a family of three in 41 states and affect 60 percent of the children currently receiving AFDC.

(b) Improve Work Incentives: The following provisions would assist families struggling to become self-sufficient while working at very low wages to support their families.

(1) Education and Training Program for Pregnant Women and Mothers with Young Children: Encourages comprehensive education, training, and employment programs for pregnant women and mothers with children under six on AFDC by providing grants to states for the development of programs in which eligible mothers may voluntarily participate. The programs will be designed to meet the individual needs of participants, and include a range of support services, like child care, at an estimated cost of $400 million.

(2) Tax Credit Exemption: Provides work incentive for AFDC recipients by requiring states to disregard the Earned Income Tax Credit (EITC) refund from countable income in determining eligibility and benefit levels. The EITC is specifically designed to help low income working families, but the current policy of treating it as income for AFDC purposes is counterproductive and creates an inequity between AFDC working families and other poor working families. The estimated cost of this provision is $50 million.

(3) Child Care Funds: See Section 2(a)(8).

(4) Eliminate Time Limit on Work Incentives: Allows AFDC recipients with very low paying jobs to supplement their income with a partial AFDC grant for the full duration of their employment, rather than limiting work incentives as is now the case. This will cost approximately $300 million.

(c) Extend Aid to Adolescents and Others with Special Needs: The following provisions recognize the special help adolescents, including teen parents, need in order to support themselves and their families.

(1) Eliminate Provisions Which Penalize Families Where Minor Parents Reside with Their Parents: Encourages family

stability by repealing the provision that requires the deeming of a grandparent's income to a grandchild for purposes of AFDC eligibility and benefit levels even when the grandparent is not contributing to the child's support. Also repeals a provision that requires the inclusion of all parents and minor siblings, except step siblings and Supplemental Security Income (SSI) recipients, in the AFDC unit. These provisions are particularly detrimental to adolescent mothers attempting to provide adequate care for their young children by residing with parents or other family members, and their elimination will cost approximately $140 million.

(2) Aid for High School and Vocational School Students 18 and Over: Encourages graduation from high school and vocational school by requiring states to continue AFDC benefits to children in school through age 20. This will allow many low-income disadvantaged students to complete their education at a cost of approximately $160 million.

(3) Aid for Pregnant Women: Encourages infant health by requiring states to provide AFDC to pregnant women with no other children from the point the pregnancy is medically verified, rather than allowing coverage only from the sixth month. This will make prenatal care more likely and help ensure adequate nutrition and shelter during the pregnancy at a cost of approximately $30 million.

(d) Two-Parent Families: The following provisions require that all states implement the AFDC Unemployed Parent Program and take steps to minimize the negative impact of AFDC requirements for children living with stepparents.

(1) Coverage of Families Under the AFDC-Unemployed Parent Program: Helps children in needy families where both parents are unemployed by requiring states to provide assistance, with a state option for revising categorical restrictions that limit coverage. This will help families stay together and ensure family stability at an estimated cost of $1.2 billion.

(2) Fairer Treatment of Stepparents: Conforms treatment of stepparent income in determining AFDC eligibility and benefit levels more closely to that of other AFDC family members. Currently some of a stepparent's income must be deemed available to the AFDC unit with which he is residing regardless of his actual contribution or legal obligation to do so. This provision will increase the amount the stepparent is allowed to disregard for his own support, and allows stepparents employed part time—as well as those employed full time—the full $75 work expense deduction applied to other workers in the AFDC unit. The provision is estimated to cost no more than $50 million.

SECTION 7: TAX REFORM:

The federal tax system places a large and growing burden on those least able to pay—working families in poverty. Single parent families and large families are hardest hit as they struggle to support their families on low wages. This section includes a number of proposals to relieve the federal tax burden on low-income working families and bring greater fairness and equity to the federal tax system.

(a) Tax Relief for Working Families: Provides tax assistance to low income working families by expanding and indexing the Earned Income Tax Credit (EITC). Eligibility for the EITC would be extended to families earning up to $16,000 per year, the maximum credit increased to $800, and the EITC indexed to maintain the value of the increase in future years. The provision would cost about $3 billion when fully implemented.

(b) Tax Relief for Working Families with Children: Provides tax relief to families with children by increasing the EITC for eligible families by $50 for each dependent child, and by an additional $50 for each child under six. The provision also requires states to disregard the EITC refunds from countable income in determining AFDC eligibility and benefit levels. The total cost is approximately $470 million.

(c) Tax Relief for Single-Parent Working Families: Provides tax relief for many female-headed families who pay disproportionately higher taxes than two-parent families by increasing the zero bracket amount (or standard deduction) for heads of households to the amount allowed for married couples filing jointly. This provision would cost about $1 billion in 1986.

(d) Dependent Care Tax Credit: Helps families with child care expenses by increasing the maximum Dependent Care Tax Credit to 50 percent of expenses and by making the credit refundable. This change costs approximately $700 million.

SECTION 8: EMPLOYMENT AND TRAINING:

Employment and training are critical incentives for economically disadvantaged youth to avoid early parenthood and to become self-sufficient adults. Yet thousands of young adults, including teens at risk of pregnancy and those with children of their own, do not have adequate skills or training to secure jobs that will allow them to support themselves and their families. This section expands the successful components of the Job Training Partnership Act (JTPA) so that more adolescents and young adults receive the basic training, support services, work experience, and wages necessary for self-sufficiency.

(a) Job Training Partnership Act (JTPA): Assists economically disadvantaged adults and youth to secure training and employment by providing $4.7 billion (an increase of $700 million) for programs under Title II-A of JTPA with special efforts to recruit youths at risk of adolescent pregnancy, youths from public assistance families, and adolescent parents, and increase the funds set aside for child care and transportation services nec-

essary for effective participation. This provision would also improve coordination between JTPA programs and other educational programs such as Basic Adult Education and Vocational Education.

(1) Summer Youth Employment Program: Ensures individualized youth programs by converting existing summer youth employment programs to a program that combines a youth's basic academic and remedial education activities with work experience, and appropriating $824 million (an increase of $100 million) for JTPA Title II-B, the Summer Youth Employment Program. Provision also requires each Private Industry Council to contribute a percentage of local funds in order to obtain additional federal funds above the amount available in the preceding fiscal year.

(2) Job Corps: Serves additional disadvantaged youth by providing $700 million (an increase of $100 million) for JTPA Title IV-B Corps.

(b) Minimum Wage Level: Helps low income working families by increasing the current minimum wage from $3.35 to $4.00 an hour. This change would reflect the 20 percent inflation since January 1981 when the minimum wage was last adjusted.

Title II: Reform and Elimination of Tax Subsidies and Weapons Systems

This title proposes the elimination of several large tax subsidies that have allowed wealthy individuals and corporations to escape their fair share of federal taxes. For example, 128 major and profitable American corporations paid no federal income taxes in at least one of the last three years, and many actually received substantial refunds from the federal government. These changes, many proposed by the U.S. Department of Treasury, will ensure a more equitable tax system, and together with the elimina-

tion of the MX missile system will contribute over $40 billion to the federal treasury in the 1986 fiscal year. This is more than enough to finance the preventive investments in children and families proposed in Title I, while reducing the deficit by more than $25 billion.

(a) Luxuries: Reinstates the 10 percent excise tax on jewelry, furs, and other luxury items repealed in 1967, contributing $2.5 billion to the federal treasury.

(b) Liquor: Restores the excise tax on alcoholic beverages to the percentage amount levied in 1951. Currently the percentage has dropped by one half, and doubling it contributes $3.8 billion to the federal treasury.

(c) Cigarettes: Doubles the tax on cigarettes from 16 cents to 32 cents per pack rather than cutting the tax in half as is scheduled to take place this year. This proposal would help discourage smoking—especially among adolescents and pregnant women—and would contribute about $5 billion to the federal treasury.

(d) Boats: Places a 10 percent excise tax on the sale of all recreational boats and would contribute about $100 million.

(e) Business Meals and Entertainment: Excludes the cost of business expense account meals, entertainment, and travel as proposed by the U.S. Department of Treasury, adding $1.5 billion to federal revenues. At a time when children and families are giving up meals essential to minimal health and nutrition, fiscal austerity should also extend to business meals and entertainment.

(f) Excessive Write-offs for Corporate Investment: Repeals two of the largest, interrelated tax breaks for corporations—the accelerated cost recovery system and the investment tax credit—and replaces them with depreciation rules that are based on the actual cost to the companies. The U.S. Department of the Treasury recently recommended this change,

which will add $18 billion in federal revenues the first year, and additional revenues thereafter.

(g) Oil Extraction Tax Shelter: Repeals the excess percentage depletion and intangible drilling expenses, one of the largest tax shelters for the oil industry. Repeal of this shelter will add $6.8 billion to the federal treasury the first year, with additional revenue in future years.

(h) Capital Gains Tax on Large Estates: Eliminates a tax break for people who inherit large estates—the automatic exemption from capital gains tax on the long-term assets—contributing $1 billion to the federal treasury.

(i) MX Missile System: Eliminates the MX missile system, saving $2.5 billion in FY 1986. The preponderance of evidence indicates the costly MX missile system can be eliminated without threat to national security. While the same may be true of other weapons systems, elimination of the MX is necessary in light of the critical needs of children and adolescents. □

PART **2**

1
BLACK AND WHITE CHILDREN AND THEIR FAMILIES

There were 62.1 million children under age 18 living in 30.8 million families in 1984: 15.1 percent of the children and 10.6 percent of the families were black, 81.5 percent of the children and 87.0 percent of the families were white.

For most white children, family means a mother and a father. This is not true for most black children.

- Eight out of every 10 white children live in two-parent families; only 4 out of 10 black children do.

- Black children are 3 times more likely than white children to live in households headed by someone other than one or both of their parents. One black child in 5 lives in such a household.

- Black children are three and one-half times more likely than white children to live in female-headed households. Half of the black children in America live in female-headed households.

- One-fourth of America's black children live with a parent who has never married. Only 1 white child in 48 lives with a never-married parent.

- The proportion of children living in female-headed families more than doubled between 1960 and 1984 (see fig. 1). Today, 1 child in 5 lives in such a family. The proportion doubled for both blacks and whites. For black children, however, this means that half now live in families headed by women.

Fig. 1 Percentage of Children Living in Female-Headed Families, 1960 and 1984

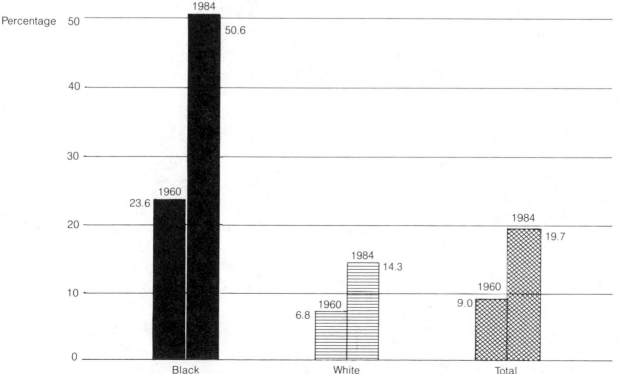

93-412

■ There are over 62.1 million children living in the United States: 15.1 percent are black, 81.5 percent are white.

TABLE 1.1

Children in the United States, by Age and Race, March 1984 (in millions)

Age	Black	White	Total
Under 3	1.75	8.73	10.84
Under 6	3.33	17.14	21.21
Under 18	9.38	50.63	62.14

Source: U.S. Department of Commerce, Bureau of the Census, *Current Population Reports,* Series P-60, No. 145, "Money Income and Poverty Status of Families and Persons in the United States: 1983 (Advance Data From the March 1984 Current Population Survey)" (Washington, D.C., August 1984), table 17. Calculations by Children's Defense Fund.

Note: Table excludes children who are institutionalized.

Children under age 18 make up 33.9 percent of the black population, 25.6 percent of the white population, and 26.8 percent of the total population. In 1960, 42.5 percent of the population was under age 18.

Data on children in America's 170 largest cities in appendix, table 29.

■ The total number of children will increase to 67.4 million by the year 2000: 16.9 percent will be black.

TABLE 1.2

Projected Number of Children in the United States, by Age and Race, 1985-2000 (in millions)

Race and Age	1985	1990	1995	2000
Black children	9.66	10.26	11.04	11.40
Under 6	3.61	3.85	3.81	3.70
6-13	3.90	4.47	5.07	5.15
14-17	2.15	1.94	2.16	2.55
White children	51.19	51.91	53.74	53.51
Under 6	17.72	18.44	17.87	16.73
6-13	21.32	22.93	24.48	24.47
14-17	12.15	10.55	11.38	12.31
All children	62.84	64.34	67.13	67.39
Under 6	22.03	23.00	22.47	21.27
6-13	26.08	28.39	30.58	30.74
14-17	14.73	12.95	14.08	15.38
Percentage of children who are black	15.4%	15.9%	16.4%	16.9%
Percentage of children age 6-13	41.5	44.1	45.6	45.6
Children as a percentage of total population	26.3	25.8	25.9	25.1

Source: U.S. Department of Commerce, Bureau of the Census, *Current Population Reports*, Series P-25, No. 952, "Projections of the Population of the United States, by Age, Sex, and Race: 1983 to 2080" (Washington, D.C., May 1984), table 6. Calculations by Children's Defense Fund.

The major growth in the number of children will be in the 6- to 13-year-old age group, which will comprise 45.6 percent of the under-18 population by the year 2000. Children will comprise 25.1 percent of the total population by that time.

■ There are over 61.3 million families in the United States: 10.6 percent are black, 87.0 percent are white.

TABLE 1.3

Families in the United States, by Presence and Age of Children and Race, March 1983 (in millions)

Presence and Age of Children	Black	White	Total
Families with children	3.89	26.01	30.82
Under 6	1.77	11.59	13.80
6-17	3.05	19.24	22.99
Families without children	2.64	27.40	30.58
Total	6.53	53.41	61.39
Percentage of families with children	59.6%	48.7%	50.2%

Source: U.S. Department of Commerce, Bureau of the Census, *Current Population Reports*, Series P-20, No.388, "Household and Family Characteristics: March 1983" (Washington, D.C., May 1984), table 1. Calculations by Children's Defense Fund.

Black families are somewhat more likely than white families to have children. Six out of 10 black families have children.

Data on the number of families and children, 1940-2000, in appendix, table 1.

■ Only 4 black children in 10 live with both parents. Eight out of 10 white children live in two-parent families. More than half the black children in America live only with their mothers. One black child in 18 lives with neither parent.

TABLE 1.4

Family Living Arrangements of Children, by Age and Race, March 1983

Age and Family Living Arrangement	Black	White	Total
Children under 18			
Living with both parents	40.7%	81.0%	74.9%
Living with mother only	51.1	15.0	20.5
Living with father only	2.5	2.0	2.0
Living with relative, but not with either parent	4.9	1.6	2.1
Living with nonrelative or not in household	0.8	0.4	0.5
Children under 3			
Living with both parents	37.7	85.5	77.6
Living with mother only	57.2	12.1	19.5
Living with father only	1.6	1.4	1.4
Living with relative, but not with either parent	2.7	0.7	1.0
Living with nonrelative or not in household	0.8	0.4	0.4

Source: U.S. Department of Commerce, Bureau of the Census, *Current Population Reports*, Series P-20, No. 389, "Marital Status and Living Arrangements: March 1983" (Washington, D.C., June 1984), table 4.

The proportion of black children living only with their mothers increased from 41.9 percent to 51.1 percent between 1979 and 1983. Part of this increase was due to a decline in the number of two-parent families, which fell from 43.4 percent in 1979 to 40.7 percent in 1983. Most of the change, however, was due to a drop in the number of children living in relatives' households without a parent present. This figure dropped from 11.3 percent in 1979 to 4.9 percent in 1983.

Data on marriage and divorce by individual year, 1940-1983, in appendix, table 2.

■ The proportion of children in female-headed families more than doubled for both blacks and whites between 1960 and 1984. This increase had a greater effect on black children. In 1960, about one-fourth of black children were in female-headed families; in 1984, half were.

TABLE 1.5

Percentage of Children Living in Female-Headed Families, by Race, 1960-1984

Year	Black	White	Total
1960	23.6%	6.8%	9.0%
1970	33.7	7.8	11.3
1980	49.8	13.1	18.6
1984	50.6	14.3	19.7

Source: U.S. Department of Commerce, Bureau of the Census, *Current Population Reports*, Series P-60, No. 145, "Money Income and Poverty Status of Families and Persons in the United States: 1983 (Advance Data From the March 1984 Current Population Survey)" (Washington, D.C., August 1984), table 15. Calculations by Children's Defense Fund.

■ One black child in 4 lives with a parent who has never married. One white child in 48 lives with a never-married parent.

TABLE 1.6

Percentage of Children with an Absent Parent, by Cause and Race, March 1983

Reason for Parent's Absence	Black	White	Total
Never married	24.1%	2.1%	5.4%
Separated	13.3	3.7	5.2
Divorced	12.2	9.0	9.4
Widowed	2.9	1.5	1.8
Other reason[a]	1.0	0.6	0.7
Neither parent lives with child[b]	5.7	2.0	2.6
Total with absent parent	59.3	19.0	25.1

Source: U.S. Department of Commerce, Bureau of the Census, Current Population Reports, Series P-20, No. 389, "Marital Status and Living Arrangements: March 1983" (Washington, D.C., June 1984), tables 4 and 5. Calculations by Children's Defense Fund.

[a]For example, a parent in the armed services.

[b]The marital status of the child's parents is unknown.

Black children are 3 times more likely than white children to have an absent parent. They are almost 12 times more likely to live with a parent who has never married.

In 1970, only 4.6 percent of black children lived with a parent who had never married. The percentage had tripled to 13.2 percent by 1980. In the 3 years between 1980 and 1983, however, the percentage rocketed to 24.1. There was a parallel trend for white children, but the percentages were very small; only 2 white children in 100 lived with a never-married parent in 1983.

Data for children with an absent parent, 1970 and 1980, in appendix, table 3.

■ Black children are 3 times more likely than white children to live in households headed by someone other than one of their parents. One black child in 5 lives in such a household.

TABLE 1.7

Relationship of Children to Family Head, by Age and Race, March 1983

Age and Relationship to Family Head	Black	White	Total
Children under 18			
Own child	81.1%	94.3%	92.2%
Grandchild or other relative[a]	17.1	4.4	6.4
Not related or not in a household	1.8	1.3	1.4
Children under 3			
Own child	70.0	91.7	88.1
Grandchild or other relative[a]	28.0	7.1	10.6
Not related or not in a household	2.1	1.2	1.3

Source: U.S. Department of Commerce, Bureau of the Census, *Current Population Reports*, Series P-20, No. 389, "Marital Status and Living Arrangements: March 1983" (Washington, D.C., June 1984), table 4. Calculations by Children's Defense Fund.

[a]One or both of the child's parents may or may not also live with the child, but neither parent is reported as the family head.

Thirty percent of black children under age 3 live in households headed by someone other than their parents.

2
CHILDREN WITHOUT HOMES

Black children are more likely than white children to live away from their parents or relatives.

- Black children are 3 times more likely to be in foster care than are white children. Over 100,000 black children were in foster care in 1980.

- Black children remain in foster care far longer than do white children; almost one-third of the black children in foster care have been there over 5 years.

- Black children are about twice as likely as white children to be living in institutions. They are 4 times more likely to be living in correctional institutions.

- Black children who are not living in institutions but are away from their families live in group quarters at 4 times the rate of white children.

■ Almost 10 percent of America's black children are in families supervised by a child welfare agency, 4 times the supervision rate for white children. Black children are 3 times more likely than white children to live away from their families.

TABLE 2.1

Children under Child Welfare Supervision, 1980

	Black	White	Total
All children under child welfare supervision	822,961 (10.7%)	1,172,455 (2.7%)	2,185,066 (3.7%)
In own home[a]	722,716 (9.4%)	997,356 (2.3%)	1,874,123 (3.2%)
In out-of-home placement	100,245 (1.3%)	175,099 (0.4%)	310,943 (0.5%)
Percentage of children under supervision who are in out-of-home care	12.2%	14.9%	13.8%

Source: U.S. Department of Health and Human Services, Office for Civil Rights, *1980 Children and Youth Survey of Public Welfare and Social Services Agencies, Directory of Agencies* (Washington, D.C., 1981), table 1. Calculations by Children's Defense Fund.

[a]As of July 1, 1980.

Note: Figures in parentheses are the percentage of all children in the race group.

■ Black children remain in foster care far longer than do white children. Almost one-third of the black children in foster care have been there for over 5 years.

TABLE 2.2

Length of Time in Out-of-Home Placement, by Age and Race, 1980

Length of Time	Black	White	Total
Under 1 year	26.8%	38.6%	34.2%
1-3 years	26.6	29.6	28.6
3-5 years	14.6	12.7	13.4
Over 5 years	31.3	18.6	23.2

Source: U.S. Department of Health and Human Services, Office for Civil Rights, *1980 Children and Youth Survey of Public Welfare and Social Services Agencies, Directory of Agencies* (Washington, D.C., 1981), table 1. Calculations by Children's Defense Fund.

■ Black children are about twice as likely as white children to be living in institutions. They are 4 times more likely to be in correctional institutions.

TABLE 2.3

Children in Institutions, by Race, 1980 (per 100,000 children)

Placement	Black	White	Total
Mental hospital	33.31	24.97	25.86
Correctional institution	46.47	10.92	16.93
Other institutions[a]	335.69	181.94	210.68

Source: U.S. Department of Commerce, Bureau of the Census, *1980 Census of Population, Volume 1, Characteristics of the Population, Chapter D, Detailed Population Characteristics, Part 1, United States Summary,* PC80-1-D1-A (Washington, D.C., May 1984), table 266. Calculations by Children's Defense Fund.

[a]Includes homes for the mentally retarded, physically handicapped, etc.

More detailed data on children in institutions in appendix, tables 4 and 5.

■ Over 360,000 children live with nonrelatives or in group quarters. Black children are 4 times more likely than white children to live in group quarters.

TABLE 2.4

Children Not Living with Relatives or in Institutions, by Age, Residential Arrangement, and Race, March 1982

Age and Arrangement	Black	White	Total
Under 3			
In households	6,000	22,000	28,000
In group quarters	7,000	12,000	19,000
3-5			
In households	9,000	14,000	23,000
In group quarters	2,000	17,000	19,000
6-14			
In households	19,000	53,000	54,000
In group quarters	20,000	33,000	54,000
15-17			
In households	6,000	112,000	122,000
In group quarters	6,000	11,000	17,000
Total under 18			
In households	39,000	201,000	256,000
In group quarters	35,000	72,000	108,000
Percentage of all children under 18			
In households	0.4%	0.4%	0.4%
In group quarters	0.4	0.1	0.2

Source: U.S. Department of Commerce, Bureau of the Census, *Current Population Reports*, Series P-20, No. 389, "Marital Status and Living Arrangements: March 1982" (Washington, D.C., May 1983), table 4. Calculations by Children's Defense Fund.

Note: Group quarters are noninstitutional living arrangements for groups living in housing units with 5 or more persons unrelated to the person in charge. A household includes all persons who occupy a housing unit. In this table, household refers to 4 or fewer persons sharing a home; the child in question is unrelated to any of those persons.

3
CHILDREN HAVING CHILDREN

Over 56 percent of all births to black women were out of wedlock in 1982. Almost 9 out of 10 babies born to black women under age 20 were born outside of marriage, about two and one-half times the out-of-wedlock rate for white teenage mothers.

- There were 523,000 births to teenagers in 1982: 146,000 or 27.9 percent of these births were to black teens.

- Black teenagers accounted for almost 6 out of 10 of the births to teens under age 15.

- Births to unmarried black teens occur 5 times more often than births to unmarried white teens. However, the birth rates for black teens and black unmarried teens have been declining while the rates for white teens have been increasing in recent years. In 1970, births to unmarried black teens occurred 9 times more often than births to unmarried white teens.

- The proportion of black women who are mothers by the time they are age 20 has increased slightly since 1940, from 40 to 44 percent. What has changed dramatically is the frequency with which black teens marry. Since 1957, the marriage rate for pregnant 15 to 17 year olds has dropped about 75 percent. The rate for black 18 to 19 year olds is down about 62 percent (see fig. 2).

Fig. 2　Percentage of Women with a Premaritally Conceived First Birth Who Married before the Birth

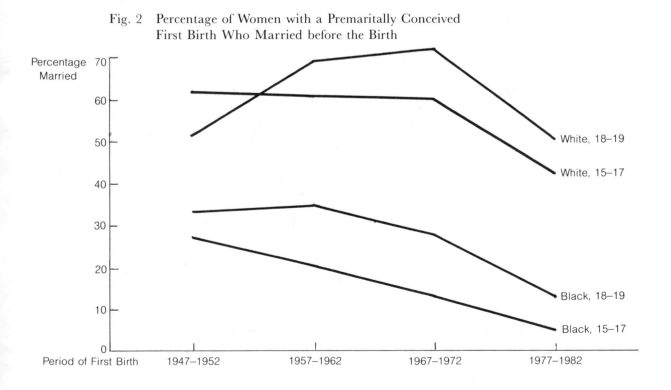

■ There were 523,000 births to teenagers in 1982: 146,000 or 27.9 percent of these births were to black teens. Teenage births accounted for 24.6 percent of all births to black women and 12.1 percent of all births to white women that year.

TABLE 3.1

Births, by Age of Mother and Race, 1982

Age	Black	White	Total
Under 15	5,395	4,153	9,773
15-19	140,534	357,948	513,758
15-17	60,282	115,869	181,162
18-19	80,252	242,079	332,596
20-24	207,640	958,509	1,205,979
25-29	143,748	961,053	1,151,934
30-34	69,781	503,847	605,273
35-39	21,341	136,664	167,920
40+	4,202	19,880	25,900
Total	592,641	2,942,054	3,680,537
Percentage of all births that are to women under 20	24.6%	12.1%	14.2%

Source: U.S. Department of Health and Human Services, National Center for Health Statistics, *Monthly Vital Statistics Report*, Vol. 33, No. 6, Supplement, "Advance Report of Final Natality Statistics, 1982" (Washington, D.C., September 28, 1984), table 2. Calculations by Children's Defense Fund.

The number of births to adolescents has declined steadily since the early 1970s, when it peaked at over 650,000.

Black teenagers accounted for 58.5 percent of the births to teens under age 15 in 1982.

Overall birth rates by race and individual year, 1940-1983, and projected birth rates, 1986-2000, in appendix, table 6.

■ Black teens are twice as likely as white teens to become pregnant. They are more likely to become pregnant unintentionally. Faced with an unintended pregnancy, they are more likely to have the child. Thirty-nine out of 100 black teens with an unintended pregnancy actually have a baby, compared to 25 out of 100 white teens.

TABLE 3.2

Pregnancy Rates[a] For Women Ages 15 to 19, by Pregnancy Outcome and Race, 1980

Outcome	Black	White	Total
Live births	95	45	53
Abortions	66	38	43
Fetal deaths	25	13	15
Total pregnancies	185	96	111
Percentage of pregnancies resulting in			
Live births	51%	47%	48%
Abortions	36	40	39

[a]Per 1,000 women ages 15 to 19.

Source: The Alan Guttmacher Institute, *Information on Fertility Patterns: Focus on Black Adolescents* (New York, N.Y., 1984), table 9.

More data on pregnancy rates in appendix, tables 6 and 7.

TABLE 3.3

Pregnancy Rates[a] For Unintended Pregnancies For Women Ages 15 to 19, by Pregnancy Outcome and Race, 1980

Pregnancy Outcome	Black	White	Total
Live births	53	15	21
Abortions	66	38	43
Fetal deaths	17	7	9
Total pregnancies	135	60	73
Percentage of unintended pregnancies resulting in			
Live births	39%	25%	29%
Abortions	49	64	59
Percentages of all pregnancies that are unintended	73%	63%	66%

[a]Per 1,000 women ages 15 to 19.

Source: The Alan Guttmacher Institute, *Information on Fertility Patterns: Focus on Black Adolescents* (New York, N.Y., The Alan Guttmacher Institute, 1984), table 9.

■ One black 15- to 19-year-old woman out of 10 gave birth in 1982, more than twice the rate of young white women. Birth rates for black adolescents have been declining steadily since 1970, when 1 black adolescent in every 7 gave birth.

TABLE 3.4

Birth Rates for 15- to 19-Year-Old Women, by Race, 1970-1982 (live births per 1,000 15- to 19-year-old women)

Year	Black	White	Total
1970	140.6	57.4	68.3
1971	134.5	53.6	64.5
1972	129.8	51.0	61.7
1973	123.1	49.0	59.3
1974	116.5	47.9	57.5
1975	111.8	46.4	55.6
1976	104.9	44.1	52.8
1977	104.7	44.1	52.8
1978	100.9	42.9	51.5
1979	101.7	43.7	52.3
1980	100.0	44.7	53.0
1981	97.1	44.6	52.7
1982	97.0	44.6	52.9

Source: U.S. Department of Health and Human Services, National Center for Health Statistics, *Monthly Vital Statistics Report*, Vol. 33, No. 6, Supplement, "Advance Report of Final Natality Statistics, 1984" (Washington, D.C., September 28, 1984), table 4.

The birth rate for white teens declined from 1970 to 1978, but it has been rising ever since.

More detailed data on births to adolescent women, 1950–1982, in appendix, table 8.

■ Black teens account for 27.9 percent of all births to teenagers, but for 47.3 percent of all births to unmarried teens. In 1982, 127,500 births were to unmarried black teenagers, 5,300 were to black teens under age 15.

TABLE 3.5

Births to Unmarried Women, by Age of Mother and Race, 1982

Age of Mother	Black	White	Total
Under 15	5,305	3,225	8,720
15-19	122,163	130,677	260,626
20-24	122,126	126,882	257,473
25-29	56,349	58,054	118,954
30-34	22,202	25,162	49,559
35-39	6,469	9,173	16,420
40 +	1,313	2,007	3,475
Total	335,927	355,180	715,227
Percentage of all births that are to women under 20	37.9%	37.7%	37.7%

Source: U.S. Department of Health and Human Services, National Center for Health Statistics, *Monthly Vital Statistics Report*, Vol. 33, No. 6, Supplement, "Advance Report of Final Natality Statistics, 1982" (Washington, D.C., September 28, 1984), table 17.

Although the number of births to adolescents has declined steadily since 1970, the proportion of these births that are to unmarried teens has been increasing. In 1950, 13.9 percent of adolescent births were out of wedlock. By 1970, this percentage had more than doubled to 30.5. In 1982, it rose to 51.5 percent (see appendix, table 8).

The upward trend in adolescent out-of-wedlock births parallels a general rise in births to single women. In fact, while the proportion of teen births that are out of wedlock has been growing, teen out-of-wedlock births have been making up smaller percentages of the total births to unmarried women. Teens accounted for about 53 percent of all births outside marriage in 1973. They made up 38 percent in 1982 (see appendix, table 9).

■ Almost 9 out of every 10 babies born to black teens are born out of wedlock, about two and one-half the white out-of-wedlock rate. Among black women in general, however, out-of-wedlock rates are very high. More than half the children born to black women of all ages are born to single mothers, compared to 12.1 percent of the children born to white women. Since 1970, the proportion of babies born to single women has almost doubled; among whites, the proportion has more than doubled. These increases can be seen at all age levels. For some groups of white women, the proportion has almost tripled.

TABLE 3.6

Birth Ratios to Unmarried Women, by Age of Mother and Race, 1970-1982

Year and Age	Black	White	Total
1970			
Under 15	93.5%	57.9%	80.8%
15-19	62.7	17.1	29.5
20-24	31.3	5.2	8.9
25-29	20.3	2.1	4.1
30-34	19.6	2.1	4.5
35-39	18.6	2.7	5.2
40 +	18.3	3.3	5.7
Total, all ages	37.6	5.7	10.7
1980			
Under 15	98.5%	75.4%	88.7%
15-19	85.2	33.0	47.6
20-24	56.0	11.5	19.4
25-29	36.2	5.0	9.0
30-34	29.2	4.5	7.5
35-39	28.1	6.3	9.4
40 +	29.3	8.5	12.1
Total, all ages	55.3	11.0	18.4
1982			
Under 15	98.3%	77.7%	89.2%
15-19	86.9	36.5	50.7
20-24	58.8	13.2	21.4
25-29	39.2	6.0	10.3
30-34	31.8	5.0	8.2
35-39	30.3	6.7	9.8
40 +	31.3	10.1	13.4
Total, all ages	56.7	12.1	19.4

Sources: U.S. Department of Health, Education, and Welfare, National Center for Health Statistics, *Vital and Health Statistics,* Series 21, No. 36, "Trends and Differentials in Births to Unmarried Women: United States, 1970-76" (Washington, D.C., 1980), table H; U.S. Department of Health and Human Services, National Center for Health Statistics, *Monthly Vital Statistics Report,* Vol. 31, No. 8, Supplement, "Advance Report of Final Natality Statistics, 1980" (Washington, D.C., November 30, 1982), table 15; and U.S. Department of Health and Human Services, National Center for Health Statistics, *Monthly Vital Statistics Report,* Vol 33, No. 6, Supplement, "Advance Report of Final Natality Statistics, 1982" (Washington, D.C. September 28, 1984), table 17.

■ Births to unmarried black teens occur 5 times more often than births to unmarried white teens. The birth rate for black unmarried teens has generally been decreasing since 1970 while the rate for unmarried white teens has been rising.

TABLE 3.7

Birth Rates for 15- to 19-Year-Old Unmarried Women, by Race, 1970-1981 (live births per 1,000 unmarried 15- to 19-year-old women)

Year	Black	White	Total
1970	96.9	10.9	22.4
1971	98.6	10.3	22.3
1972	98.2	10.4	22.8
1973	94.9	10.6	22.7
1974	93.8	11.0	23.0
1975	93.5	12.0	23.9
1976	89.7	12.3	23.7
1977	90.9	13.4	25.1
1978	87.9	13.6	24.9
1979	91.0	14.6	26.4
1980	89.2	16.2	27.6
1981	86.8	17.1	28.2
1982	87.0	17.7	28.9

Source: U.S. Department of Health and Human Services, National Center for Health Statistics, *Monthly Vital Statistics Report*, Vol. 33, No. 6, Supplement, "Advance Report of Final Natality Statistics, 1982" (Washington, D.C., September 28, 1984), table 18.

Data on birth rates for unmarried women, ages 15 to 44, by age groups, individual years, and race in appendix, table 10.

■ There has been a sharp decline in the marriage rate of young black women who conceived outside of marriage. Over a 20-year period, since the late 1950s, the marriage rate for these women dropped 74.1 percent for 15 to 17 year olds and 61.6 percent for 18 and 19 year olds. White rates are down by about one-third.

TABLE 3.8

Percentage of Women with Premaritally Conceived First Births Who Married before the Birth, by Age and Race, 1947-1982 (in 5-year periods)

Race and Period of First Birth[a]	Age at First Birth 15-17	Age at First Birth 18-19	Age at First Birth 20-24
Black women			
1947-1952	27.2%	33.3%	b
1952-1957	33.3	—b	31.1
1957-1962	20.1	34.4	23.1
1962-1967	18.8	40.8	30.1
1967-1972	13.4	27.7	28.0
1972-1977	7.7	19.0	16.7
1977-1982	5.2	13.2	10.8
White women			
1947-1952	62.3	51.9	64.0
1952-1957	61.3	69.0	68.1
1957-1962	61.0	69.5	67.3
1962-1967	62.0	68.4	68.9
1967-1972	60.1	72.5	65.4
1972-1977	53.5	59.4	55.8
1977-1982	42.7	50.1	52.0

Source: U.S. Department of Commerce, Bureau of the Census, *Current Population Reports*, Series P-20, No. 387, "Fertility of American Women: June 1982" (Washington, D.C., April 1984), table F.

[a]Periods are from July of beginning year to June of final year.

[b]Numbers too small to compute a reliable percentage.

■ Teen mothers are less likely than older mothers to have completed high school. Only 53.9 percent of teenagers who gave birth at age 18 or 19 had completed high school, compared to 77.3 percent of women who gave birth in their early twenties. Among teenage mothers, 15 to 17 years old, giving birth in 1981, less than 10 percent had completed school.

TABLE 3.9

Percentage of Births to Young Mothers Who Completed 12 or More Years of School, by Marital Status, Age, and Race, 1981

Marital Status and Age of Mother	Black	White	Total
Births to married women			
15-17	15.6%	11.2%	11.4%
18-19	61.6	55.9	56.2
20-24	80.1	81.4	81.0
Births to unmarried women			
15-17	8.9	8.0	8.5
18-19	54.7	46.7	50.7
20-24	66.7	59.0	63.2
Births to all women			
15-17	9.2	9.7	9.5
18-19	55.9	53.3	53.9
20-24	72.2	78.8	77.3

Source: U.S. Department of Health and Human Services, National Center for Health Statistics, *Vital and Health Statistics*, Series 21, No. 41, "Trends in Teenage Childbearing, 1970-1981" (Washington, D.C., September 1984), table 8.

More data on educational achievement and marital status in appendix, table 11.

4
INCOME AND POVERTY

Black children are more likely than white children to live in low-income families. Black and white single-parent families and black families with heads under age 25 or with older heads are also especially likely to be low income.

• The median family income of black families is less than six-tenths that of white families. Half of all black families had incomes below $14,500 in 1983.

• Almost half of all black children are poor. One white child in 6 is poor. Children make up 36.6 percent of the white population living below poverty. They comprise an even larger proportion of the poor black population. Over 4 out of every 10 poor blacks are children.

• Black children in two-parent families are twice as likely as white children in two-parent families to live below the poverty line.

• Black children in female-headed families are the poorest in the nation. Half live in families with incomes below $6,100. Between 1977 and 1982, the median incomes of these children's families dropped 28.3 percent, a far greater decline than was suffered by any other group of children, black or white (see fig. 3).

• Whether black or white, young mothers under age 25 heading families are very likely to be poor. The poverty rates in 1983 were 85.2 percent for young black female-headed families and 72.1 percent for young white female-headed families. But black female-headed families are much more likely to stay poor. In female-headed families with older mothers, ages 25 to 44, there is a 25 percentage points gap between black and white poverty rates.

Fig. 3   Median Family Incomes of Children

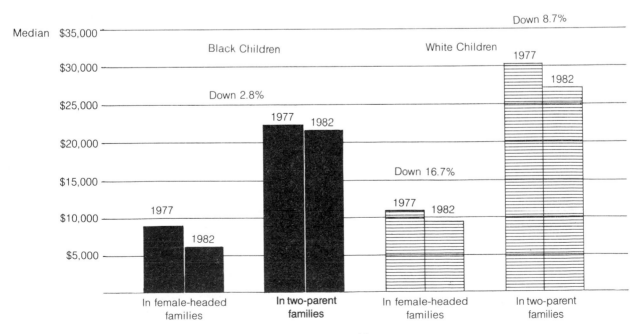

■ The median family income of black families is less than 60 percent that of white families. Half of America's black families had incomes below $14,500 in 1983.

TABLE 4.1

Median Family Income, by Race, 1970-1983 (in 1983 dollars)

Year	Black	White	Total	Black Income as Percentage of White Income
1970	$16,111	$26,263	$25,317	61.3%
1983	$14,506	$25,757	$24,580	56.3%
Percentage change 1970-1983	− 10.0%	− 1.9%	− 2.9%	

Source: U.S. Department of Commerce, Bureau of the Census, *Current Population Reports*, Series P-60, No. 145, "Money Income and Poverty Status of Families and Persons in the United States: 1983 (Advance Data from the March 1984 Current Population Survey)" (Washington, D.C., August 1984), table 3.

Median family income, in real dollars, was less in 1983 than it was in 1970. Black family income has lost ground relative to white family income: the median family income of black families was 10.0 percent less in 1983 than it was in 1970, 5 times the decline among white families.

Data for median family income by individual years, 1970-1983, in appendix, table 12.

■ Part of the income gap between black and white families can be attributed to the fact that black families are three and one-half times more likely than white families to be headed by women. Regardless of family type, however, black families earn significantly less than white families.

TABLE 4.2

Median Family Income, by Type of Family and Race, 1983

Type of Family	Black	White	Total	Black Income as Percentage of White Income
Husband-wife	$21,840	$27,691	$27,286	78.9%
Wife in labor force	26,389	32,569	32,107	81.0
Wife not in labor force	13,821	22,359	21,890	61.8
Female-headed	7,999	13,761	11,789	58.1
Male-headed	15,552	23,208	21,845	67.0
All families	14,506	25,757	24,580	56.3

Source: U.S. Department of Commerce, Bureau of the Census, *Current Population Reports*, Series P-60, No. 145, "Money Income and Poverty Status of Families and Persons in the United States: 1983 (Advance Data from the March 1984 Current Population Survey)" (Washington, D.C., August 1984), table 1.

In families in which there is only one worker, whether or not there is a spouse present, black families earn at least one-third less than white families. The median family income of blacks approaches that of whites only when both husband and wife work. Half of these black families still earn less than $26,389, four-fifths the median family income of white two-worker families.

For both black and white families, working wives make a significant contribution to family income. Among blacks, however, this contribution is more substantial. The median family income of two-worker black families is almost twice that of families in which the wife is not in the labor force. Among white husband-wife families, a working wife increases a family's earnings by almost one-half.

■ Regardless of family type, black families are about twice as likely as white families to live in poverty. More than half the black families headed by women are poor.

TABLE 4.3

Types of Families below the Poverty Level, by Race, 1983

Type of Family	Black		White		Total	
	Number	Percentage	Number	Percentage	Number	Percentage
Husband-wife	533,000	15.5%	3,135,000	6.9%	3,820,000	7.6%
Female-headed	1,545,000	53.8	1,920,000	28.3	3,557,000	36.0
Male-headed	84,000	23.7	168,000	10.4	264,000	13.0
All families	2,162,000	32.4	5,223,000	9.7	7,641,000	12.3

Source: U.S. Department of Commerce, Bureau of the Census, *Current Population Reports*, Series P-60, No. 145, "Money Income and Poverty Status of Families and Persons in the United States: 1983 (Advance Data From the March 1984 Current Population Survey)" (Washington, D.C., August 1984), tables 14 and 15.

Note: The poverty level in 1983 was $10,178 for a family of 4.

Female-headed families are almost 5 times more likely than husband-wife families to be poor.

Overall, black families live in poverty at more than 3 times the rate of white families. Part of this difference, however, is due to the large number of black female-headed families.

■ Children are the poorest group in American society. More than 1 child out of 5 was poor in 1983. More than half the children in female-headed families were poor; over two-thirds of the children in black female-headed families were poor.

TABLE 4.4

Children Living in Poverty, by Race and Family Structure, 1983 (in millions)

	Black		White		Total	
	Number	*Percentage*	*Number*	*Percentage*	*Number*	*Percentage*
Children living in families	4.26	46.3%	8.46	16.9%	13.33	21.7%
Female-headed	3.19	68.5	3.36	46.9	6.71	55.4
Other (including two-parent)	1.07	23.6	5.10	11.9	6.62	13.4
Children under age 18[a]	4.38	46.7	8.78	17.3	13.81	22.2
All persons	9.89	35.7	23.98	12.1	35.27	15.2
Children as percentage of all poor persons		44.3		36.6		39.2

Source: U.S. Department of Commerce, Bureau of the Census, *Current Population Reports*, Series P-60, No. 145, "Money Income and Poverty Status of Families and Persons in the United States: 1983 (Advance Data from the March 1984 Current Population Survey)" (Washington, D.C., August 1984), tables 15 and 17.

[a]Includes children not in families.

A child in a female-headed family is 4 times more likely to be poor than a child in a male-headed or two-parent family.

Forty-four percent of the poor blacks in the United States are children. Children make up a smaller proportion of the white population below poverty.

More detailed data on children and families in poverty in appendix, tables 13, 14 and 15.

■ Black children in female-headed families are the poorest in the nation. They saw a 28.3 percent decline in their families' incomes between 1977 and 1982, far greater than the declines suffered by any other group of children, black or white.

TABLE 4.5

Median Family Income among Children, by Family Structure and Race, 1977 and 1982 (in 1982 dollars)

Family Structure and Year	Black	White	Total
Children in two-parent families			
1982	$21,949	$27,380	$26,831
1977	22,570	30,003	29,423
Percentage change 1977-1982	− 2.8%	− 8.7%	− 8.8%
Children in female-headed families			
1982	6,108	9,246	7,912
1977	8,518	11,100	9,954
Percentage change 1977-1982	− 28.3%	− 16.7%	− 20.5%
Children in all families			
1982	11,667	24,538	23,017
1977	14,203	27,931	26,284
Percentage change 1977-1982	− 17.9%	− 12.1%	− 12.4%

Sources: U.S. Department of Labor, Bureau of Labor Statistics, unpublished data from the March 1978 Current Population Survey and from the March 1983 Current Population Survey. Calculations by the Children's Defense Fund.

Real median family income for all children declined by more than 12 percent between 1977 and 1982. Black children were more severely affected than were white children. Children in female-headed families were hurt more than children in two-parent families. Black children in two-parent families were the least affected, those in female-headed families, the most affected.

■ Black children in female-headed families benefited least from the anti-poverty efforts of the 1960s. Eight out of 10 of these children lived in poverty in 1959. The proportion was down to about 6 out of 10 in 1979. By 1983, it was up to almost 7 out of 10.

TABLE 4.6

Percentage of Children in Poverty, by Family Structure and Race, 1959-1983

Family Structure and Year	Black	White	Total
Female-headed families			
1959	81.6%	64.6%	72.2%
1969	68.2	45.2	54.4
1979	63.1	38.6	48.6
1982	70.7	46.5	56.0
1983	68.5	46.9	55.4
Percentage change 1959-1979[a]	− 22.7	− 40.2	− 32.7
Percentage change 1979-1983[a]	+ 8.6	+ 21.5	+ 14.0
Two-parent and male-headed families			
1959	60.6%	17.4%	22.4%
1969	25.0	6.7	8.6
1979	18.7	7.3	8.5
1982	24.1	11.6	13.0
1983	23.6	11.9	13.4
Percentage change 1959-1979[a]	− 69.1	− 58.0	− 62.1
Percentage change 1979-1983[a]	+ 26.2	+ 63.0	+ 57.6

Sources: U.S. Department of Commerce, Bureau of the Census, *Current Population Reports*, Series P-60, No. 145, "Money Income and Poverty Status of Families and Persons in the United States: 1983 (Advance Data from the March 1984 Current Population Survey)" (Washington, D.C., August 1984), table 15; and U.S. Department of Commerce, Bureau of the Census, *Current Population Reports*, Series P-60, No. 125, "Money Income and Poverty Status of Families and Persons in the United States: 1979 (Advance Report)" (Washington, D.C., October 1980), table 18. Calculations by Children's Defense Fund.

[a]A negative change means an improvement in the poverty situation, a positive change means a worsening.

Poverty rates for children in all types of families declined between 1959 and 1979. The major reductions took place among two-parent and male-headed families. The poverty rate for black children in such families dropped from 60.6 percent to 18.7 percent; the rate for white children dropped from 17.4 percent to 7.3 percent.

Since 1979, the poverty rate for all children, regardless of race or family structure, has risen dramatically. The increase has been greatest for white children in two-parent families. They are and always have been the least likely to be poor, but their poverty rate increased from 7.3 percent to 11.9 percent between 1979 and 1983, a 63.0 percent rise.

■ Whether black or white, young mothers under age 25 heading families are very likely to be poor. The poverty rates in 1983 were 85.2 percent for young black female-headed families and 72.1 percent for young white female-headed families. But black female-headed families are much more likely to stay poor; 62.6 percent of black female-headed families with older mothers, ages 25 to 44, live in poverty. Among whites, the rate drops to 38.1 percent.

TABLE 4.7

Percentage of Families with Children under Age 18 with 1982 Incomes below the Poverty Level, by Age of Family Head, Family Type, and Race, March 1983

Family Type and Age of Head	Black	White	Total
Two-parent families	17.2%	9.0%	9.8%
Under 25	25.8	18.9	19.5
25-44	13.6	8.5	9.0
Female-headed families	63.7	39.3	47.8
Under 25	85.2	72.1	77.7
25-44	62.6	38.1	46.1

Source: U.S. Department of Commerce, Bureau of the Census, *Current Population Reports*, Series P-60, No. 144, "Characteristics of the Population below the Poverty Level: 1982" (Washington, D.C., March 1984), table 19.

■ Female-headed families with children are 9 times more likely than those without children to fall below the poverty line.

TABLE 4.8

Percentage of Young Families[a] with 1982 Incomes below the Poverty Level, by Family Type and Presence of Children, March 1983

Family Type and Presence of Children	Black	White	Total
Married couples	24.2%	11.4%	12.4%
With children	25.8	18.9	19.5
With no children	—[b]	3.7	4.6
Female-headed families	82.6	62.9	70.4
With children	85.2	72.1	77.7
With no children	—[b]	—[b]	8.5

Source: U.S. Department of Commerce, Bureau of the Census, *Current Population Reports*, Series P-60, No. 144, "Characteristics of the Population below the Poverty Level: 1982" (Washington, D.C., March 1984), table 6.

[a]Families with heads under age 25.

[b]Based on fewer than 75,000 families; poverty rates not calculated.

The difference in poverty rates between childless families and families with children is smaller among married-couple families but still striking. A married couple with at least 1 child is 4 times more likely than a childless couple to be poor.

■ White mothers living with their children by an absent father are twice as likely as black mothers in this situation to be awarded child support. They are also twice as likely actually to receive child support.

TABLE 4.9

Recipients of Child Support Payments, by Race, 1981

	Black	*White*	*Total*
Mothers awarded child support	33.8%	69.2%	59.2%
Mothers actually receiving child support	23.9	57.6	48.2

Source: U.S. Department of Commerce, Bureau of the Census, *Current Population Reports*, Series P-23, No. 124, "Child Support and Alimony: 1981 (Advance Report)" (Washington, D.C., May 1983), table 1. Calculations by Children's Defense Fund.

■ Over 50 percent of all AFDC families are white. Approximately 80 percent of all AFDC families have only one adult recipient, and the majority of these are mothers. Two-thirds of all recipients are children, half of them are white.

TABLE 4.10

Families and Children Receiving AFDC, 1979

	Number	*Percentage*
Families	3,428,078	
White	1,771,785	51.7%
Black	1,503,595	43.9
With 1 child	1,456,838	42.5
With 2 children	959,984	28.0
With 3 children	532,654	15.5
With 4 or more children	476,618	13.9
With no adult recipient	509,953	14.9
With 1 adult recipient	2,704,558	78.9
With 2 adult recipients	211,583	6.2
Individual recipients	10,651,794	—
Children	7,230,304	67.9
Living with mother	6,720,697	—
Living with father	814,528	—
White	3,554,111	—
Black	3,302,653	—
Adults	3,421,490	32.1

Source: U.S. Department of Health and Human Services, Social Security Administration, *Aid to Families with Dependent Children: 1979 Recipient Characteristics Study, Part 1, Demographic and Program Characteristics* (Washington, D.C., 1982), tables 1, 2, 3, 4, 5, 13, 14, 18, 20, 25, and 34.

5
EMPLOYMENT AND UNEMPLOYMENT

Black children are more likely than white children to have at least one parent who is unemployed, and, paradoxical as it may seem, they are more likely to have a mother who works full time. As teenagers they are more likely to be unemployed than are white teens.

- Black children are more than twice as likely as white children to have no parent employed and almost 4 times more likely to have no parent in the labor force.

- The unemployment rate of black teens is almost 3 times that of whites. Only 2 black youths out of 10 hold jobs.

- Young black college graduates have about the same chance of being unemployed as white high school dropouts. Their unemployment rate is more than 3 times the rate for white college graduates (see fig. 4).

Fig. 4   Unemployment Rates of 16 to 24 Year Olds
Not Enrolled in School, October 1982

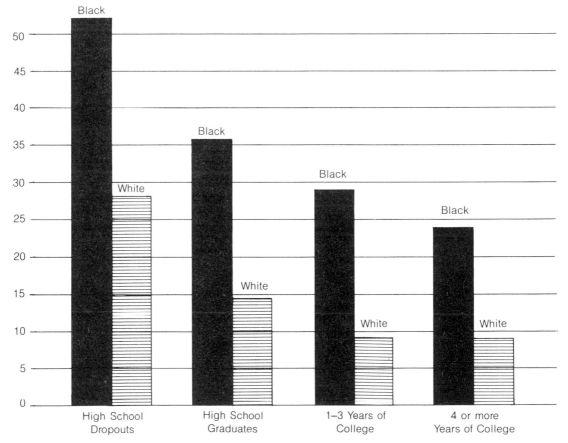

■ Only 67.0 percent of America's black children have an employed parent; 86.0 percent of white children have at least one working parent. Black children are more than twice as likely as white children to have no parent employed and almost 4 times more likely to have no parent in the labor force.

TABLE 5.1

Percentage of Children Affected by Parental Unemployment, by Race, March 1979 and March 1984

Employment Status of Parent	Black 1979	Black 1984	White 1979	White 1984	Total 1979	Total 1984
At least one parent currently employed[a]	69.5%	67.0%	90.4%	89.4%	88.4%	86.0%
At least one parent currently unemployed[b]	10.1	15.4	5.7	8.2	6.3	9.2
At least one parent currently unemployed and none employed[b]	6.2	9.1	2.4	3.9	2.9	6.6
No parent in the labor force[c]	24.3	23.9	6.1	6.6	8.6	9.3

Sources: U.S. Department of Labor, Bureau of Labor Statistics, unpublished data from the March 1979 and March 1984 Current Population Surveys. Calculations by Children's Defense Fund.

[a]Parents in armed forces counted as employed.

[b]A child with two parents, one employed and one unemployed, will be counted twice, once in each of these categories.

[c]A parent who is neither currently employed nor seeking work is counted as not in the labor force. Most such parents are female heads of young or large families.

Between 1979 and 1984, there was a 3.6 percent drop in the proportion of black children with at least one employed parent, over 3 times the drop among white children.

More detailed data on family structure, income, and labor force participation for 1984 in appendix, table 16.

■ At all ages, black men and women are more likely to be unemployed than white men and women. In September 1984, about 15 percent of all blacks were unemployed compared to about 6 percent of all whites. Almost half the black teens looking for work were unable to find jobs.

TABLE 5.2

Unemployment Rates of the Civilian Population, by Age, Race, and Sex, September 1984 (not seasonally adjusted)

Age	Black Males	Females	White Males	Females
16-19	43.7%	48.2%	16.1%	16.3%
20-24	28.3	24.0	8.7	8.5
25-29	12.7	15.8	5.3	6.8
30-34	7.8	12.0	4.4	6.2
35-44	8.6	9.2	4.5	5.6
45-54	8.0	9.8	3.6	4.6
55-64	7.8	6.0	4.2	4.6
65 and over	9.3	5.4	2.5	3.2
Total	14.8	15.2	5.6	6.6
25-54	9.3	11.5	4.4	5.8

Source: U.S. Department of Labor, Bureau of Labor Statistics, *Employment and Earnings*, Vol. 31, No. 10 (Washington, D.C., October 1984), table A-4.

■ Blacks were more likely to be employed than were whites in 1900. Black and white men were employed at equal rates, and black women were employed at twice the rate for white women—2 black women in 5 were employed. Today, at most ages, black and white women are equally likely to be employed, and black men are consistently less likely to be employed than are white men. Overall, whites are now more likely to be employed than are blacks.

TABLE 5.3

Employment Ratios, by Age, Sex, and Race, 1900 and 1983

Age and Year	Males		Females	
	Black	White	Black	White
16-24				
1900	89.0%	83.4%	47.9%	29.1%
1983	38.7	62.9	30.2	56.3
25-34				
1900	95.4	96.4	41.8	17.3
1983	71.7	86.7	58.8	63.5
35-44				
1900	96.5	96.6	41.6	12.7
1983	77.6	89.8	64.4	64.0
45-54				
1900	97.0	95.4	42.2	11.7
1983	74.9	86.6	56.1	58.4
55-64				
1900	95.5	89.5	41.0	10.8
1983	55.7	66.1	41.6	39.2

Sources: U.S. Department of Commerce and Labor, Bureau of the Census, *Bulletin*, No. 8, "Negroes in the United States" (1904), table LIX; and U.S. Department of Labor, Bureau of Labor Statistics, *Employment and Earnings*, Vol. 31, No. 1 (Washington, D.C., January 1984), table 3. Calculations by Children's Defense Fund.

■ Black men and women at all ages are less likely to be employed than white men and women, and those who are employed earn less than their white counterparts. The most important income differences, however, are between white males and other workers. Among 45 to 49 year olds, there is a $10,000 to $15,000 gap between white males' median incomes and those of blacks and women.

TABLE 5.4

Median Total 1982 Incomes of Full-Time, Full-Year Workers, by Age, Sex, and Race

| Age | Black | | White | |
	Male	Female	Male	Female
20-24	$10,647	$10,079	$12,920	$10,990
25-29	13,955	12,781	18,847	14,055
30-34	17,452	14,403	21,960	15,040
35-39	18,455	13,056	25,293	15,508
40-44	17,145	13,514	26,211	14,653
45-49	16,520	11,472	26,406	14,565
All ages	15,790	12,376	22,232	13,847

Source: U.S. Department of Commerce, Bureau of the Census, *Current Population Reports*, Series P-60, No. 142, "Money Income of Households, Families, and Persons in the United States: 1982" (Washington, D.C., February 1984), table 46.

The median income earned by white male 45 to 49 year olds is more than twice that earned by white male 20 to 24 year olds. Black males' earnings increase only 55 percent over this age spread, having peaked between ages 35 and 39.

Black women's earnings are highest between ages 30 and 34. This peak is only $4,300 more than the median income of 20- to 24-year-old black women.

■ In general, education facilitates employment, but at each educational level blacks are more likely to be unemployed than are whites. Black high school graduates are more than twice as likely as white high school graduates to be unemployed—1 in 5 black men and 1 in 6 black women are unemployed. Black male college graduates are unemployed at 3 times the rate of white male college graduates.

TABLE 5.5

Unemployment Rates for All Persons over Age 15, by Education, Race, and Sex, March 1984

| Years of Education | Black | | White | |
	Male	Female	Male	Female
Less than 8	18.0%	14.7%	12.8%	13.1%
8	17.0	14.7	11.6	12.0
9-11	28.9	25.1	15.7	14.5
12 (high school graduate)	20.0	16.7	8.2	6.5
13-15	10.7	13.0	5.2	5.0
16 (college graduate)	9.4	6.9	3.1	2.9
17+	4.4	2.9	2.1	1.7
Total	18.7	15.7	7.6	6.6

Source: U.S. Department of Labor, Bureau of Labor Statistics, unpublished data from the March 1984 Current Population Survey.

■ Black men and women at all educational levels are less likely to be employed than are white men and women, and those who are employed tend to earn less. The most striking differences are between white males and other workers. In 1982, white male college graduates earned a median income of $29,000, black male graduates earned $19,000, white female graduates earned $18,000, and black female graduates earned $16,000.

TABLE 5.6

Median Money Income in 1982 of Full-Time, Full-Year Workers over Age 24, by Years of Education, Sex, and Race

Years of Education	Black		White	
	Male	*Female*	*Male*	*Female*
Less than 8	$11,288	$10,346	$12,762	$ 8,176
8	13,462	8,199	16,773	10,572
9-11	15,104	10,353	18,203	10,803
12 (high school graduate)	16,469	12,105	21,856	13,458
13-15	18,839	15,177	24,179	15,721
16 (college graduate)	18,829	16,183	28,745	17,596
17 +	25,204	21,112	32,542	21,474
All levels	16,534	12,674	23,549	14,734

Source: U.S. Department of Commerce, Bureau of the Census, *Current Populations Reports*, Series P-60, No. 142, "Money Income of Households, Families, and Persons in the United States: 1982" (Washington, D.C., February 1984), table 47.

The white male with an advanced degree earns almost $20,000 more than the white male with less than an eighth grade education; the black male earns only $14,000 more than the black male with an eighth grade education. Black and white women receive about the same returns on their educational investments.

■ Blacks and women are over-represented in low-paying occupations and under-represented in high-paying occupations. Six out of 10 black men are in occupations with median weekly earnings below $300. Six out of 10 white men are in occupations with median weekly earnings above $300. Black women are 4 times more likely than white women to be in private household jobs paying an average of $131 per week.

TABLE 5.7

Occupational Groups of Employed Persons over Age 15, by Race and Sex, March 1984

Occupations	Black		White	
	Male	*Female*	*Male*	*Female*
Executive, administrative, and managerial ($477)[a]	6.6%	4.9%	13.8%	9.1%
Professional ($450)	5.8	11.2	12.4	15.3
Technical and related ($388)	2.0	3.4	2.8	3.4
Skilled production and trades ($387)	14.2	2.2	20.5	2.2
Protective services ($359)	4.2	0.7	2.3	0.4
Sales ($309)	5.2	7.4	12.0	13.1
Operators, Transportation, and Laborers ($285)	33.7	14.2	19.7	9.2
Clerical, administrative support ($273)	8.4	25.4	5.4	29.6
Service, excluding protective service and private household ($203)	15.3	24.2	6.3	15.2
Agricultural ($200)	4.3	0.5	4.6	1.1
Private household ($131)	0.4	5.9	0.0	1.5
Percentage in occupations with median weekly earnings				
Above $400	12.4	16.1	26.2	24.4
Below $300	62.1	70.2	36.0	56.6

Sources: U.S. Department of Labor, Bureau of Labor Statistics, unpublished data from the March 1984 Current Population Survey; and U.S. Department of Labor, Bureau of Labor Statistics, News Release USDL 84-326, "Earnings of Workers and their Families: Second Quarter 1984" (Washington, D.C., July 30, 1984), table 5. Calculations by Children's Defense Fund.

[a]The figures in parentheses are the median weekly earnings for the adjacent occupations.

■ The unemployment rate of black teenagers is almost 3 times that of white teenagers. Almost half the black teens in the labor force are unable to find jobs: only 2 out of 10 currently hold jobs.

TABLE 5.8

Youth Employment and Unemployment, by Age, Race, and Sex, March 1984 (not seasonally adjusted)

Age, Race, and Sex	Percentage of Population Employed	Unemployment Rate
16–19		
Black	20.5%	45.8%
Male	23.0	43.7
Female	18.0	48.2
White	45.9	16.2
Male	47.0	16.1
Female	44.9	16.3
20–24		
Black	51.6	26.3
Male	57.3	28.3
Female	46.7	24.0
White	71.9	8.6
Male	78.0	8.7
Female	65.9	8.5

Source: U.S. Department of Labor, Bureau of Labor Statistics, *Employment and Earnings*, Vol. 31, No. 10 (Washington, D.C., October 1984), table A-4. Calculations by Children's Defense Fund.

Unemployment rates of young adults, 20 to 24 years old, are lower than those of teens, but black rates are still 3 times those of whites. One-fourth of the black 20 to 24 year olds who want jobs are unable to find them.

■ Young black college graduates have an unemployment rate almost as high as that of white high school dropouts: about 1 out of 4 cannot find jobs. Among black high school dropouts the picture is much worse: more than half are unemployed.

TABLE 5.9

Unemployment Rates of 16 to 24 Year Olds Not Enrolled in School, by Highest Level of Education Completed, October 1978 and October 1982

| Highest Level of School Completed | Black | | White | |
	1978	1982	1978	1982
Not high school graduate	23.1%	52.9%	16.5%	27.8%
High school graduate	21.9	35.7	7.0	14.6
1-3 years of college	16.5	28.4	4.5	8.9
4 years or more of college	15.1	23.9	5.7	8.6
Total	23.1	38.6	8.3	15.7

Source: U.S. Department of Labor, Bureau of Labor Statistics, *Special Labor Force Reports*, No. 223, "Students, Graduates, and Dropouts in the Labor Market, October 1978" (Washington, D.C., 1980), table J; and U.S. Department of Labor, Bureau of Labor Statistics, *Monthly Labor Review*, Vol. 106, No. 8 (Washington, D.C., August 1983), p. 30. Calculations by Children's Defense Fund.

Unemployment rates for all youths, black and white, rose markedly between 1978 and 1982, roughly doubling among high school graduates and those with some college education.

Among college graduates, blacks were harder hit than whites: the unemployment rate for black college graduates jumped from 15.1 percent in 1978 to 23.9 percent in 1982. The unemployment rate for white college graduates rose nearly 51 percent, from 5.7 percent to 8.6 percent.

■ Young workers, black and white, earn significantly less than older workers. Employed black 16 to 24 year olds earn two-thirds of the median $278 per week that older black workers earn. Employed white 16 to 24 year olds earn about 60 percent of the median $355 per week earned by older white workers.

TABLE 5.10

Median Weekly Earnings of Full-Time Workers, by Age, Race, and Sex, 1983

Race and Sex	Age 16-24	Age 25 +	Young Workers' Earnings as Percentage of Older Workers' Earnings
Black	$185	$278	66.5%
Male	193	309	62.5
Female	180	245	73.5
White	208	355	58.6
Male	227	409	55.5
Female	201	268	75.0
Total	207	349	59.3
Male	223	405	55.1
Female	201	263	76.4

Source: U.S. Department of Labor, Bureau of Labor Statistics, unpublished data.

Young women, black and white, earn about 75 percent of what women over age 24 earn. This reflects the fact that women's earnings do not increase significantly with age.

■ The earning power of young workers relative to older workers has declined over the last 15 years. In 1967, black 16 to 24 year olds earned 81.7 percent of what older black workers earned. Young white workers earned 72.3 percent of older white workers' earnings.

TABLE 5.11

Percentage of Older Workers' Median Weekly Earnings Earned by Full-Time Workers, Age 16 to 24, by Race and Sex, 1967 to 1983

Year	Black			White		
	Male	Female	All	Male	Female	All
1967	76.3%	100.0%	81.7%	74.8%	92.6%	72.3%
1970	82.2	100.0	86.4	69.3	90.8	71.8
1975	70.3	81.6	73.8	63.5	80.3	65.1
1980	67.2	79.8	72.8	61.4	78.2	64.5
1983	62.5	73.5	66.5	55.5	75.0	58.6

Source: U.S. Department of Labor, Bureau of Labor Statistics, unpublished data. Calculations by Children's Defense Fund.

Note: Data before 1980 are for nonwhites rather than blacks. For 1967 to 1975, data are median usual weekly earnings for full-time wage and salary workers in May of the designated year; 1980 and after are annual averages of quarterly medians. There have been several technical changes in computing the medians over the years.

■ Young married couples, black and white, have about two-thirds the cash income of all married couples. Young females heading families are even further behind. Young white women hold their families together with 39.7 percent of the income all white women have; young black women maintain families on 58.7 percent of all black women's incomes.

TABLE 5.12

Median Family Money Income, by Family Structure, Age of Householder, and Race, 1982

Family Structure and Age of Householder	Black	White	Total
Married-couple families			
All ages	$20,586	$26,443	$26,019
18-24	13,991	17,676	17,368
As percentage of income for all married-couple families	68.0%	66.8%	66.8%
Female-headed families			
All ages	$ 7,458	$13,496	$11,484
18-24	4,377	5,355	4,916
As percentage of income for all female-headed families	58.7%	39.7%	42.8%
All families			
All ages	$13,599	$24,603	$23,433
18-24	6,291	15,705	14,317
As percentage of income for all families	46.3%	63.8%	61.1%

Source: U.S. Department of Commerce, Bureau of the Census, *Current Population Reports*, Series P-60, No. 142, "Money Income of Households, Families, and Persons in the United States: 1982" (Washington, D.C., February 1984), table 23.

Among female-headed families, young black women's cash incomes are 58.7 percent of all black women's incomes; young white women's cash incomes are 39.7 percent of all white women's incomes. The difference reflects not the greater earning power of young black women, but the extremely low incomes of older black women. Almost two-thirds of black women, ages 25 and over, who head families live below the poverty line.

6
MATERNAL EMPLOYMENT AND CHILD CARE

Well over half of all children, black and white, have mothers in the labor force. Maternal employment rates for black and white mothers have converged over the last decade as more white mothers have entered the labor force, but some important differences remain in the structure and employment patterns of black families that have clear implications for the day care needs of black children.

- Black mothers play a crucial role in determining their families' incomes. Among children in families with annual incomes of $25,000 or more, more than 8 out of 10 black children under age 6 have working mothers; about half of all young white children in such families have mothers in the labor force (see fig. 5).

- Black women enter or return to the labor force when their children are younger, and they are more likely to work full time. As a result, more black children need full-time care—and at earlier ages—than do white children.

- Black and white 3 to 5 year olds are about equally likely to be enrolled in preschool programs. Black preschoolers, however, are enrolled in full-day programs at 2 to 3 times the rates for white preschoolers.

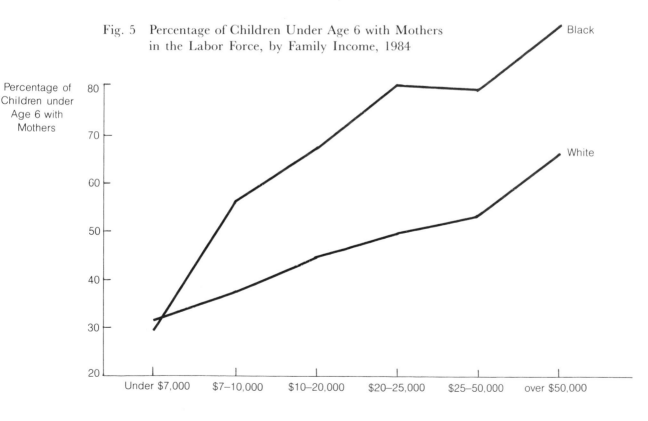

Fig. 5   Percentage of Children Under Age 6 with Mothers in the Labor Force, by Family Income, 1984

■ Black children, regardless of age, are more likely than white children to have working mothers. This is particularly true for black preschoolers. Fifty-five percent of black children under age 6 have working mothers; 47.3 percent of white children under 6 have working mothers.

TABLE 6.1

Percentage of Children with Mothers in the Labor Force, by Age and Race, 1970 to 1984

Age and Year	Black	White	Total
Under 6			
1970	42.9%	26.3%	28.5%
1974	45.1	31.1	32.9
1979	49.6	41.1	42.2
1984	55.0	47.3	48.2
6-17			
1970	52.1	44.8	43.2
1974	51.9	44.9	45.9
1979	58.7	54.7	55.2
1984	63.0	60.0	60.3
Total under 18			
1970	49.1	37.1	38.8
1974	49.9	40.9	42.1
1979	56.2	50.7	51.4
1984	60.4	55.8	56.3

Sources: U.S. Department of Labor, Bureau of Labor Statistics, *Handbook of Labor Statistics* (Washington, D.C., December 1983), table 55; U.S. Department of Labor, Bureau of Labor Statistics, News Release USDL 84-321, "Number of Working Mothers Now at Record Levels" (Washington, D.C., July 26, 1984), tables 3 and 4; and U.S. Department of Labor, Bureau of Labor Statistics, unpublished data from the March Current Population Survey, various years. Calculations by Children's Defense Fund.

Data for children with mothers in the labor force by individuals years, 1970-1984, in appendix, table 17.

Black children, particularly those under age 6, were much more likely than white children to have working mothers in 1970. The gap has narrowed considerably since then as white mothers have entered the labor force in increasing numbers. For school-age children, the gap has almost disappeared.

■ Black mothers with children under age 5 are much more likely to be employed full time than are white mothers with young children. Four out of 5 employed black mothers with preschoolers work full time, compared to 3 out of 5 white mothers.

TABLE 6.2

Percentage of Employed Women with One or More Children under Age 5 Who Work Full Time, by Race, June 1982

Employment	Black	White	Total
Full time	81.0%	60.8%	64.2%
Part time	19.0	39.2	35.8

Source. U.S. Department of Commerce, Bureau of the Census, *Current Population Reports*, Series P-23, No. 129, "Child Care Arrangements of Working Mothers: June 1982" (Washington, D.C., November 1983), table 2.

More data on labor force participation of mothers, 1947–1984, in appendix, table 18.

■ Among children in families with incomes under $7,000 a year, maternal employment rates are about the same for blacks and whites, but the gap widens as incomes increase. Among children in families earning over $25,000, 8 out of 10 black mothers work, compared to 6 out of 10 white mothers.

TABLE 6.3

Percentage of Children with Mothers in the Labor Force, by Age, Race, and Family Income, March 1984

Age and Family Income	Black	White	Total
Under 6	55.0%	47.3%	48.2%
Less than $7,000	29.9	31.9	31.0
$7,000-$10,000	56.2	37.3	39.2
$10,000-$20,000	67.4	44.4	47.3
$20,000-$25,000	80.2	49.8	52.3
$25,000-$50,000	79.4	53.4	55.3
$50,000+	93.9	56.8	58.8
6-17	63.0	60.0	60.3
Less than $7,000	42.3	38.6	39.6
$7,000-$10,000	45.8	50.0	48.4
$10,000-$20,000	70.4	59.1	60.7
$20,000-$25,000	76.0	61.0	62.5
$25,000-$50,000	82.2	64.0	65.5
$50,000+	80.8	66.1	66.7
Total under 18	60.4	55.8	56.3
Less than $7,000	37.2	35.9	36.0
$7,000-$10,000	48.8	45.2	45.1
$10,000-$20,000	69.4	53.6	55.4
$20,000-$25,000	77.3	56.8	58.8
$25,000-$50,000	81.3	60.7	62.4
$50,000+	83.9	64.2	65.0

Source: U.S. Department of Labor, Bureau of Labor Statistics, unpublished data from the March 1984 Current Population Survey. Calculations by Children's Defense Fund.

Black mothers play a crucial role in determining their families' incomes both because they are often family heads and because their husbands, when present, earn considerably less than the average white male. The high employment rates among black mothers, especially in the upper-income brackets, demonstrate their importance as wage earners.

The black-white employment gap is greatest among mothers with children under age 6. In the top income bracket, 93.9 percent of all young black children have mothers who work; 56.8 percent of young white children have mothers who work.

More detailed data on family structure, income, and labor force participation for 1984 in appendix, table 16. More data on marital and parental status of the labor force, 1983, in appendix, table 19.

■ Young black children in two-parent families are more likely than white children to have working mothers. Among young children in female-headed families the reverse is true. White children are more likely to have mothers in the labor force.

TABLE 6.4

Percentage of Children under Age 6 Whose Mothers Work or Are Seeking Work, by Race and Family Type, March 1984

Family Type	Black	White	Total
Husband-wife	68.2%	47.4%	49.0%
Female-headed	44.7	54.3	50.3
Total[a]	55.0	47.3	48.2

Source: U.S. Department of Labor, Bureau of Labor Statistics, unpublished data from the March 1984 Current Population Survey. Calculations by Children's Defense Fund.

[a]Includes children in male-headed families.

■ Reflecting their greater need for both inexpensive and full-time child care, black working mothers are more likely than white working mothers to use child care centers or relatives to care for their preschool children.

TABLE 6.5

Types of Child Care Arrangements Used by Working Mothers with a Child under Age 5, by Race, June 1982

Child Care Provider	Black	White	Total
Mother while working	3.1%	10.3%	9.1%
Father at home	8.3	14.7	13.9
Other relative in child's own home or relative's home	44.9	26.5	29.3
Nonrelative in child's own home	1.9	6.4	5.5
Nonrelative in nonrelative's home	13.8	23.6	22.0
Day care center or preschool	20.9	13.5	14.8
Other or unknown	7.1	5.0	5.3

Source: U.S. Department of Commerce, Bureau of the Census, *Current Population Reports*, Series P-23, No. 129, "Child Care Arrangements of Working Mothers: June 1982" (Washington, D.C., November 1983), table 2-A. Calculations by Children's Defense Fund.

More information on day care center enrollment by age and race in appendix, table 20.

■ Black and white 3 to 5 year olds are about equally likely to be enrolled in preschool programs. Black preschoolers, however, are enrolled in full-day programs at 2 to 3 times the rate of white preschoolers.

TABLE 6.6

Percentage of Children, Ages 3 to 5, Attending Nursery School or Kindergarten, by Age, Length of Day, and Race, October 1980

Age and Length of Day	Black	White	Total
Age 3			
Full day	18.3%	8.6%	10.2%
Part day	8.9	18.6	17.1
Total	27.2	27.2	27.3
Age 4			
Full day	34.3	11.6	15.2
Part day	15.0	34.1	31.1
Total	49.3	45.7	46.3
Age 5			
Full day	45.6	20.9	24.9
Part day	34.3	64.9	59.8
Total	79.9	85.8	84.7
3-5			
Full day	32.5	13.7	16.9
Part day	19.3	39.0	35.8
Total	51.8	52.7	52.5

Source: U.S. Department of Education, National Center for Education Statistics, *Preprimary Enrollment: 1980* (Washington, D.C., 1982), table 3. Calculations by Children's Defense Fund.

Black children are less likely than white children to live their childhoods in good health. This is particularly true for black infants, who are less likely than white infants to be born healthy or to live out their first year of life.

7
CHILD HEALTH

- Despite what is known about the value of early and adequate prenatal care, only 6 out of 10 black babies are born to mothers who received prenatal care in the first three months of pregnancy, compared to 8 out of 10 white babies.

- Nearly 1 out of every 10 black babies is born to a mother who received no prenatal care or care only in the last trimester of pregnancy. For black mothers under age 15, this number is 2 in 10.

- Black babies are more than twice as likely as white babies to be low weight at birth (less than 5.5 pounds). Low birthweight infants are more than 20 times more likely to die in the first year of life.

The risks associated with low birthweight and other environmental factors mean that, for black babies, the infant mortality rate is about the same as it was for white babies 20 years ago (see fig. 6). Black infants die at twice the rate of white infants.

Fig. 6   Infant Mortality Rates, by Race, 1940–1980

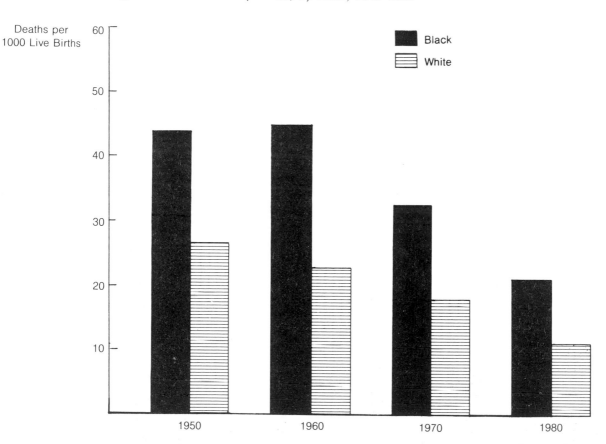

■ Black women receive less prenatal care—and receive it later in their pregnancies—than do white women. Eight out of 10 white babies are born to women who received prenatal care during their first 3 months of pregnancy, compared to only 6 out of 10 black babies. Black babies are twice as likely to be born to mothers who received late or no care (see fig. 7).

TABLE 7.1

Prenatal Care, by Race, 1982

When Prenatal Care Began	Black	White	Total
First trimester	61.5%	79.3%	76.1%
Second trimester	29.0	16.2	18.5
Third trimester	6.4	3.3	3.9
No care	3.1	1.2	1.5

Source: U.S. Department of Health and Human Services, National Center for Health Statistics, *Monthly Vital Statistics Report*, Vol. 33, No. 6, Supplement, "Advance Report of Final Natality Statistics, 1982" (Washington, D.C., September 28, 1984), table 24. Calculations by Children's Defense Fund.

Fig. 7   Babies Born to Women Who Began Prenatal Care in the First Trimester of Pregnancy, by Race, 1970–79

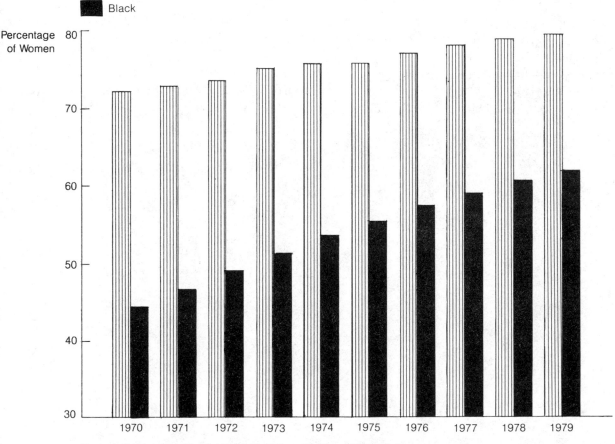

Source: National Center for Health Statistics: Division of Vital Statistics.

■ Black babies are twice as likely as white babies to be born to mothers who received late prenatal care or delivered their babies without having ever had a prenatal examination. Almost 1 black baby out of 10 is born to a mother who received late or no care. Among black teenage mothers under age 15, the proportion increases to 2 in 10.

TABLE 7.2

Percentage of Babies Born to Women Who Received Late or No Prenatal Care, by Age and Race, 1982

Age of Mother	Black	White	Total
Under 15	20.7%	21.6%	21.4%
15-19	13.7	10.2	11.3
20-24	9.7	5.2	6.1
25-29	6.9	2.7	3.4
30-34	6.3	2.4	3.1
35-39	7.5	3.9	4.5
40+	10.3	7.8	8.4
Total	9.6	4.5	5.5

Source: U.S. Department of Health and Human Services, National Center for Health Statistics, *Monthly Vital Statistics Report*, Vol. 33, No. 9, Supplement, "Advance Report of Final Natality Statistics, 1982" (Washington, D.C., September 28, 1984), table 24. Calculations by Children's Defense Fund.

The percentage of babies born to women who received late or no care increased slightly in all age groups, black and white, from 1981 to 1982. The overall rates in 1981 were 9.1 percent for blacks and 4.3 percent for whites. The most dramatic change was among very young black mothers under age 15. Their rate jumped from 18.6 percent in 1981 to 20.7 percent in 1982. The percentage of babies born to young white mothers who received late or no care did not change.

■ Black babies are more than twice as likely as white babies to be underweight at birth. One in 8 black newborns is underweight, compared to 1 in 18 white newborns. Babies born to teenage mothers are more likely to be underweight than those born to 20- to 39-year-old mothers.

TABLE 7.3

Percentage of Infants Who Are Low Birthweight, by Age of Mother and Race, 1982

Age of Mother	Black	White	Total
Under 15	15.5%	11.7%	13.8%
15-19	13.7	7.6	9.3
20-24	12.3	5.7	6.9
25-29	11.5	4.9	5.8
30-34	11.4	5.1	5.9
35-39	12.0	6.0	6.9
40-44	13.5	7.6	8.6
Total	12.4	5.6	6.8

Source: U.S. Department of Health and Human Services, National Center for Health Statistics, *Monthly Vital Statistics Report*, Vol. 33, No. 6, Supplement, "Advance Report of Final Natality Statistics, 1982" (Washington, D.C., September 28, 1984), table 15. Calculations by Children's Defense Fund.

Evidence indicates that differences in birthweight are associated with socioeconomic differences. The birthweight of black infants of higher socioeconomic status is comparable to that of whites, according to *Healthy People: The Surgeon General's Report on Health Promotion and Disease Prevention*, 1979.

Given no prenatal care, a pregnant woman is 3 times more likely to have a low birthweight child than is a pregnant woman who received prenatal care.

■ Infant mortality rates have declined steadily since 1940. Throughout this period, however, black rates have remained about twice those of whites. The infant mortality rate for blacks is about the same as it was for whites 20 years ago.

TABLE 7.4

Infant Mortality Rates, by Race, 1940-1983 (deaths per 1,000 live births)

Year	Black	White	Total
1940	72.9	43.2	47.0
1950	43.9	26.8	29.2
1960	44.3	22.9	26.0
1965	41.7	21.5	24.7
1970	32.6	17.8	20.0
1971	30.3	17.1	19.1
1972	29.6	16.4	18.5
1973	28.1	15.8	17.7
1974	26.8	14.8	16.7
1975	26.2	14.2	16.1
1976	25.5	13.3	15.2
1977	23.6	12.3	14.1
1978	23.1	12.0	13.8
1979	21.8	11.4	13.0
1980	21.4	11.0	12.5
1981	20.0	10.5	11.9
1982	—	—	11.2
1983	—	—	10.9

Sources: U.S. Congress, House of Representatives, Committee on Energy and Commerce, Subcommittee on Health and the Environment, *Infant Mortality,* Committee Print 98-J (Washington, D.C., June 1983), p. 18; U.S. Department of Health and Human Services, National Center for Health Statistics, *Monthly Vital Statistics Report*, Vol. 32, No. 12, "Births, Marriages, Divorces, and Deaths for 1983" (Washington, D.C., March 1984), p. 1; U.S. Department of Health and Human Services, National Center for Health Statistics, *Monthly Vital Statistics Report*, Vol. 33, No. 3, Supplement, "Advance Report of Final Mortality Statistics, 1981" (Washington, D.C., June 1984), table 12; and U.S. Department of Health and Human Services, National Center for Health Statistics, *Monthly Vital Statistics Report*, Vol. 32, No. 13, "Annual Summary of Births, Deaths, Marriages, and Divorces: United States, 1983" (September 21, 1984), p. 1.

■ If the black infant mortality rate in 1981 had been as low as the white rate, 5,598 fewer black infants would have died. Ten common causes of infant death accounted for two-thirds of these excess deaths. Low birthweight was the leading cause.

TABLE 7.5

Excess Black Infant Deaths When Compared to White Infant Mortality Rate, by Cause, 1981

Cause of Infant Death	Percentage of Excess Black Infant Deaths	Number of Excess Black Infant Deaths Per Year
Low birthweight	18.4%	1,030
Sudden infant death syndrome	12.8	719
Respiratory conditions	10.3	577
Respiratory distress syndrome	7.2	405
Maternal complications of pregnancy	4.9	275
Birth asphyxia	3.2	180
Pneumonia	3.1	171
Hemorrhage	2.8	156
Accidents (auto and other)	2.1	120
Perinatal infections	1.9	106
Subtotal	66.7	3,739
All other causes	33.3	1,859
Total	100.0	5,598

Source: U.S. Department of Health and Human Services, National Center for Health Statistics, *Monthly Vital Statistics Report*, Vol. 33, No. 3, Supplement, "Advance Report of Final Mortality Statistics, 1981" (Washington, D.C., June 1984), table 10. Calculations by Children's Defense Fund.

■ Black children under age 17 are less likely than white children to have visited a doctor in the preceding year.

TABLE 7.6

Percentage of Children under Age 17 Who Have Not Visited a Doctor in the Last Year, by Age and Race, 1981

Age	Black	White	Total
Under 6	14.2%	10.0%	10.9%
6-16	33.8	29.9	30.6
Total under 17	27.0	23.2	23.9

Source: U.S. Department of Health and Human Services, National Center for Health Statistics, unpublished data from the 1981 Health Interview Survey. Calculations by Children's Defense Fund.

■ One-fourth of the children under age 6 were not covered by private health insurance in 1977. Only three-fifths of blacks of all ages were covered. The poor or near poor were only half as likely to be privately insured. Insurance status also varied by occupation; the unemployed were the worst off, however.

TABLE 7.7

Percentage of Persons with Private Health Insurance Coverage, by Selected Population Characteristics, 1977

Characteristics	Percentage
Age	
Under 6	74.4%
6-18	78.2
Race	
White	84.9
Black	60.3
Hispanic	62.5
Income (adjusted for family size)	
Poor or near poor	41.0
Other low income	71.0
Middle income	86.6
High income	92.6
Occupation of family head	
Farm	78.7
Blue collar	87.0
Service	75.7
White collar	88.6
Not employed in 1977	44.3

Source: U.S. Department of Health and Human Services, National Center for Health Services Research, *National Health Care Expenditures Study,* Data Preview 17, "Private Health Insurance: Premium Expenditures and Sources of Payment" (Washington, D.C., 1984), table 1.

More data on the insurance coverage of children in appendix, table 21. More data on the insurance status of the poor and near poor in appendix, table 22. More data on the percentage of unemployed persons covered by insurance in appendix, table 23.

■ Sizeable proportions of preschool children—between 33 percent and 42 percent—are not fully immunized against one or more preventable childhood diseases. White children are far more likely to be immunized than black children are. Between 47 percent and 61 percent of black preschoolers are not fully immunized against one or more diseases.

TABLE 7.8

Percentage of 1 to 4 Year Olds Immunized against Childhood Diseases, by Race, 1982

Disease	Nonwhite	White	Total
Diphtheria-Tetanus-Pertussis	48.4%	70.6%	66.3%
Polio	39.1	62.6	58.0
Measles	53.1	66.7	64.0
Rubella	50.2	65.9	62.8
Mumps	47.8	61.5	58.9

Source: U.S. Department of Health and Human Services, Centers for Disease Control, unpublished data from the annual Immunization Survey.

■ The rate of active tuberculosis cases among nonwhite children is 4 to 5 times that of white children, regardless of age. Nonwhite groups other than black children may account for this. Southeast Asian refugee children have a high incidence of tuberculosis, for example.

TABLE 7.9

Incidence of Tuberculosis, by Age, Sex, and Race, 1979 (cases per 100,000 population)

	Nonwhite		White	
Age	Male	Female	Male	Female
Under 5	18.8	16.9	3.7	3.9
5-14	6.8	5.2	1.0	1.0
15-24	20.0	17.4	3.0	2.5

Source: U.S. Department of Health and Human Services, Centers for Disease Control, Tuberculosis in the United States, 1979 (Washington, D.C., November 1981), table 2.

■ Almost 40 percent of black children under age 17 have never visited a dentist. Half of all children under 17 have not seen a dentist in the last year, including two-thirds of the black children. Overall, white children average twice as many dental visits per year as black children.

TABLE 7.10

Dental Visits of Children under Age 17, by Race, 1981

Dental Visits	Black	White	Total
Percentage who have never visited a dentist	39.9%	30.1%	30.4%
Percentage who have not visited a dentist in the last year	64.3	44.8	50.0
Visits per year per child	0.9	1.8	1.6

Source: U.S. Department of Health and Human Services, National Center for Health Statistics, unpublished data from the 1981 Health Interview Survey. Calculations by Children's Defense Fund.

■ Breastfeeding has been shown to have nutritional, immunological, and psychological advantages, yet black mothers are only half as likely as white mothers to breast-feed their infants.

TABLE 7.11

Percentage of Newborn Infants Who Are Breastfed, by Race, 1980

Infant Feeding Method	Black	White
Bottle only	65%	40%
Breast only	25	51
Both	10	9

Source: U.S. Department of Health and Human Services, National Center for Health Statistics, unpublished data from the 1980 National Natality Survey.

Note: The data are for married women only. Unmarried women may be even less likely than married women to breast-feed their infants.

The growing appreciation of the advantages of breastfeeding have led to recent changes in infant feeding practices. The downward trend in breastfeeding, which had occurred since the 1950s, appears to have reversed in the early 1970s. However, as can be seen above, breastfeeding is not yet practiced at the same rate in all population groups.

■ Between one-fifth and one-third of black children and youths have hemoglobin levels that fall below the white median hemoglobin level. This is one indicator of poor nutritional status and anemia.

TABLE 7.12

Nutritional Status of Black Children, 1976-1980 (based on the excess percentage of black children falling below the white median hemoglobin level)

Age	Males	Females
3-5	21.1%	20.8%
6-11	22.7	29.9
12-14	23.3	28.0
15-17	26.0	32.2
18-24	26.1	26.7

Source: U.S. Department of Health and Human Services, National Center for Health Statistics, *Vital and Health Statistics*, Series 11, No. 232, "Hematological and Nutritional Biochemistry References Data for Persons 6 Months–74 Years of Age: United States, 1976-1980" (Washington, D.C., December 1982), tables 1 and 2. Calculations by Children's Defense Fund.

■ Black children are less likely than white children to use most drugs of abuse.

TABLE 7.13

Percentage of Youths Who Have Used Drugs of Abuse, by Drug, Age, and Race, 1982

Drug and Age	Black	White	Total
Marijuana			
12-17	23%	27%	27%
18-25	61	65	64
Cocaine			
12-17	n.a.	n.a.	n.a.
18-25	18	30	28
Non-medical use of prescription-type psychotherapeutic drugs[a]			
12-17	5	11	10
18-25	14	31	28

Source: U.S. Department of Health and Human Services, Alcohol, Drug Abuse, and Mental Health Administration, *National Survey on Drug Abuse; Main Findings 1982* (Washington, D.C., 1983), tables 21, 22, 34, 39 and 40.

[a]Stimulants, sedatives, tranquilizers, and analgesics.

■ The death rate for black infants is almost twice that of white infants. The decline in the black infant death rate has been less than the decline for whites.

TABLE 7.14

Infant Death Rates, by Race, 1950-1983 (deaths per 1,000 infants)

Year	Black	White	Total
1950	53.7[a]	29.9	33.0
1960	47.4	23.6	27.0
1970	38.4	18.7	21.4
1980	23.6	11.0	12.9
1981	19.9	10.6	12.1
1982	18.2	10.2	11.4
1983	18.4	9.4	10.8
Decline in 33 years	65.7%	68.7%	67.4%

Source: U.S. Department of Health and Human Services, National Center for Health Statistics, *Monthly Vital Statistics Report*, Vol. 32, No. 13, "Annual Summary of Births, Deaths, Marriages, and Divorces: United States, 1983" (Washington, D.C., September 21, 1984), table 6.

Note: The infant death rate is not the same as the infant mortality rate. The figures reported above for 1982 and 1983 are preliminary and may be revised when the final analyses are completed.

[a] The 1960 figure is for nonwhites.

■ Young black children are more likely to die than are young white children. The greatest disparity is among the youngest children.

TABLE 7.15

Child Deaths, by 5-Year Age Groups and Race, 1980 (deaths per 100,000 of children)

Age Group	Black	White	Total
Under 1 year	2,356.6	1,099.6	1,288.3
1-4	97.6	57.9	63.9
5-9	41.7	28.4	30.4
10-14	36.6	29.8	30.8
15-19	92.3	99.1	97.9

Source: U.S. Department of Health and Human Services, National Center for Health Statistics, unpublished data.

■ Older white teens are slightly more likely than older black teens to die because of their greater exposure to auto accidents and suicide. Black youths are more likely to die as a result of homicide.

TABLE 7.16

Death Rates of Children, Ages 15 to 19, by Cause of Death, Sex, and Race, 1980 (deaths per 100,000 children, ages 15 to 19)

Cause	Black Male	Black Female	White Male	White Female
Cancer	6.4	4.5	6.3	4.4
Congenital anomalies	2.0	1.0	1.5	1.2
Heart	5.9	3.9	2.2	1.4
Accident				
Automobile	24.4	6.7	69.1	25.6
Other	24.6	5.3	24.6	4.8
All other	2.1	0.9	1.7	0.5
Total all causes	134.5	50.3	142.7	53.7

Source: U.S. Department of Health and Human Services, National Center for Health Statistics, unpublished data.

■ Black youths are less than half as likely as white youths to commit suicide. White males are almost 3 times more likely than black males to commit suicide. Almost all of the increase in teenage suicides between 1973 and 1980 is concentrated among white males. The white female rate increased slightly over this period, and the rates among blacks decreased.

TABLE 7.17

Suicides among 15 to 19 Year Olds, by Sex and Race, 1973 and 1980 (deaths per 100,000 population)

Sex and Year	Black	White	Total
Male			
1980	5.6	15.0	13.8
1973	5.7	11.4	10.7
Female			
1980	1.6	3.3	3.0
1973	2.1	3.2	3.1
Total			
1980	3.6	9.2	8.5
1973	3.9	7.4	7.0

Source: U.S. Department of Health and Human Services, National Center for Health Statistics, unpublished data. Calculations by Children's Defense Fund.

■ Black children are 3 to 4 times more likely than white children to be murdered.

TABLE 7.18

Homicide Deaths, by Age and Race, 1980 (deaths per 100,000 population)

Age	Black	White	Total
Under 1 year	15.7	4.3	5.9
1-4	6.8	1.7	2.5
5-9	2.0	0.7	0.9
10-15	3.2	1.1	1.4
15-19	29.9	7.5	10.6

Source: U.S. Department of Health and Human Services, National Center for Health Statistics, unpublished data. Calculations by Children's Defense Fund.

■ Black infants are 3 times more likely than white infants to die of known child abuse, and 4 times more likely to be victims of other homicides.

TABLE 7.19

Homicide Deaths of Children under Age 1, by Race, 1980 (deaths per 100,000 population)

Cause of Death	Black	White	Total
From child abuse	5.4	1.8	2.3
Other homicide	10.3	2.5	3.5
Total known homicide	15.7	4.3	5.9
Other external causes[a]	4.9	1.4	1.9

Source: U.S. Department of Health and Human Services, National Center for Health Statistics, unpublished data. Calculations by Children's Defense Fund.

[a]Unknown whether death was accidental or intended.

8
EDUCATION

Black and white children are equally likely to be enrolled in school, but black children, for a host of reasons, are much less likely to succeed in school.

• Almost 1 black child out of 4 is growing up in a family whose head did not complete high school, twice the rate for white children. White children, on the other hand, are 3 times more likely than black children to live in families headed by college graduates.

• Black children score fewer correct answers on reading tests than do white children. The older they get, the worse they score.

• White and black children are equally likely to be in special classes in public schools—1 in 10 is in such a placement—but 6 out of 10 special placements of white students are into programs for the gifted and talented. Only 1 black placement in 10 is into these programs. Black children are 3 times more likely than white children to be placed in classes for the educable mentally retarded.

• Black students are more likely than white students to be suspended from school, corporally punished in school, behind in school, or not enrolled in school at all. In 1982, 1 black 18 to 21 year old in 4 had dropped out of school; 1 white in 7 was a high school dropout. Forty percent of the black female dropouts left school because of pregnancies (see fig. 8).

• Those black students who graduate from high school are now less likely than whites to attend college. College attendance rates were about the same for blacks and whites in 1977. Poverty is the key to low college attendance among blacks; 18.8 percent of poor black high school graduates attended college in 1983; 34.0 percent of those above poverty attended. There was only a 7 percentage point difference in the attendance rates of whites above and below the poverty line.

Fig. 8   Percentage of Recent High School Graduates Enrolled in College, 1977–1982

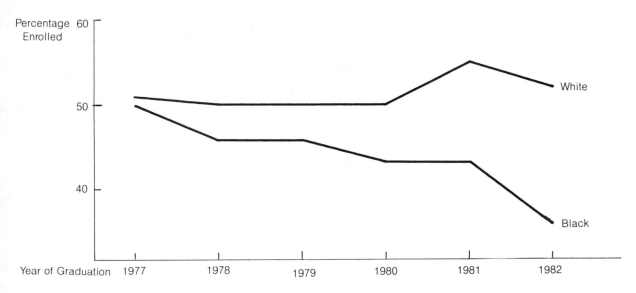

89

■ Over 5 million children were enrolled in preschool programs, 42.4 million in elementary and secondary programs, and 10.9 million in college in 1981. Blacks constituted about 15 percent of preprimary, elementary, and secondary students, and 11 percent of college students.

TABLE 8.1

School Enrollment, by Level and Race, October 1981

Level	Black	White	Total
Preprimary	758,000	4,282,000	5,719,000
Elementary	4,291,000	22,663,000	795,000
Secondary	2,168,000	12,062,000	14,642,000
College	1,133,000	9,162,000	10,734,000
Percentage full time	71.9%	70.4%	70.5%

Source: U.S. Department of Commerce, Bureau of the Census, *Current Population Reports*, Series P-20, No. 373, "School Enrollment—Social and Economic Characteristics of Students: October 1981 (Advance Report)" (Washington, D.C., February 1983), table 1.

More data on racial isolation in the public schools in appendix, table 24.

■ Virtually all American children, ages 7 through 15, are enrolled in school. The differences between blacks and whites at all age levels are very small. But these enrollment figures mask glaring differences in the education of black and white children.

TABLE 8.2

Percentage of Children Enrolled in School, by Age and Race, October 1981

Age	Black	White	Total
3-4	36.7%	35.6%	36.0%
5-6	94.5	93.9	94.0
7-9	98.8	99.3	99.2
10-13	99.4	99.3	99.3
14-15	97.1	98.1	98.0
16-17	91.3	90.4	90.6
18-19	48.2	48.5	49.0

Source: U.S. Department of Commerce, Bureau of the Census, *Current Population Reports*, Series P-20, No. 373, "School Enrollment—Social and Economic Characteristics of Students: October 1981 (Advance Report)" (Washington, D.C., February 1983), table 6.

■ Black public school students are almost twice as likely as white students to be suspended from school and are about 50 percent more likely to be corporally punished.

TABLE 8.3

Percentage of All Public School Students Suspended and Corporally Punished, by Race, Fall 1982

Disciplinary Action	Black[a]	White[a]	Total
Suspended	9.9%	5.2%	6.4%
Corporally punished	7.0	4.7	5.0

Source: U.S. Department of Education, Office for Civil Rights, "1982 Elementary and Secondary School Civil Rights Survey, National Summaries" (Washington, D.C., February 1984).

Note: Data are from a survey of 3,100 school districts taken in fall 1982. They may not be comparable to previous surveys, however, because the weights have not been adjusted to reflect the national population of schools.

[a]Excluding those of Hispanic origin.

■ Black students at all ages are poorer readers than whites. Significant gains were made by many young black students during the 1970s, but the gap still remains. There is a 19 percentage points gap between the reading scores of black and white 17 year olds.

TABLE 8.4

Average Reading Scores, by Age and Race, 1971 and 1980 (percentage of answers correct)

Age and Year	Black	White
Age 9		
1971	50%	66%
1980	60	69
Age 13		
1971	45	63
1980	50	63
Age 17		
1971	52	71
1980	52	71

Source: U.S. Congress, House of Representatives, Committee on Education and Labor, Subcommittee on Elementary, Secondary, and Vocational Education, *Oversight on State Education Statistics (Student Performance and Education Funding),* Hearings, January and February 1984, (Washington, D.C., 1984), p. 60, chart E, unpublished data from the National Assessment of Educational Progress.

■ White and black children are equally likely to be in special classes in public schools—
1 in 10 is in such a placement—but a black child is more than 3 times more likely than
a white child to be placed in a class for the educable mentally retarded and is only
one-third as likely to be admitted to a class for the gifted and talented.

TABLE 8.5

Percentage of Public School Students in Special Class Placements, by Type of Placement and Race, Fall 1982

Type of Placement	Black	White	Total
Educable mentally retarded	3.3%	1.0%	1.6%
Specific learning disabled	4.1	3.8	3.9
Severely emotionally disturbed	0.7	0.6	0.6
Trainable mentally retarded	0.4	0.3	0.3
Gifted and talented	1.4	4.1	3.2

Source: U.S. Department of Education, Office for Civil Rights, "1982 Elementary and Secondary School Civil Rights Survey, National Summaries" (Washington, D.C., February 1984). Calculations by Children's Defense Fund.

■ Black students, particularly black female students, are more likely than whites to end their high school careers in vocational rather than academic programs.

TABLE 8.6

Percentage of High School Seniors in Academic, Vocational, and General Tracks, by Race and Sex, 1982

Sex and Track	Black	White[a]	Total
Male seniors			
Academic	34.6%	39.1%	36.4%
Vocational	30.5	23.0	25.6
General	35.0	37.9	38.0
Female seniors			
Academic	34.2	42.2	39.4
Vocational	34.4	25.5	27.5
General	31.4	32.3	33.0
All high school seniors			
Academic	34.4	40.7	37.9
Vocational	32.6	24.3	26.6
General	33.0	35.0	35.5

Source: U.S. Department of Education, National Center for Education Statistics, unpublished data from High School and Beyond, 1982 Cycle.

[a]Does not include Hispanic students.

More data on high school enrollment in specific courses in appendix, table 25.

■ Black students are far more likely than white students to be behind in school. Black 17 year olds are 3 times more likely than white 17 year olds to be 2 or more years behind the modal grade for their age. Almost half the black 17-year-old males are either behind in school or have dropped out.

TABLE 8.7

Percentage of All 17 Year Olds, by Level of School Enrollment, Sex, and Race, October 1981

Sex and Level of Enrollment	Black	White	Total
Males			
In 12th grade or high school graduate	51.5%	68.3%	65.7%
In 11th grade	19.7	15.7	16.4
Below 11th grade	20.1	4.9	7.2
Dropped out	8.4	11.1	10.7
Females			
In 12th grade or high school graduate	63.3	74.7	72.7
In 11th grade	20.1	13.5	14.6
Below 11th grade	5.7	2.5	3.4
Dropped out	10.6	9.3	9.3
Total			
In 12th grade or high school graduate	57.5	71.5	69.2
In 11th grade	20.0	14.7	15.5
Below 11th grade	12.7	3.7	5.3
Dropped out	9.5	10.2	10.0

Source: U.S. Department of Commerce, Bureau of the Census, unpublished data from the October 1981 Current Population Survey. Calculations by Children's Defense Fund.

Note: A 17 year old is typically enrolled in the twelfth grade, although many have already graduated. A 17-year-old student enrolled in eleventh grade is one year behind the modal grade for age 17.

■ Because black students are more likely to be behind in school, the dropout rate for black 16 and 17 year olds is lower than that for whites. Black youths, age 18 and older, however, are about 50 percent more likely than whites to have dropped out of school. In 1982, about 1 black 18 to 21 year old out of 4 had dropped out of school.

TABLE 8.8

School Dropouts, by Age and Race, October 1982

Age	Black	White	Total
16-17	6.0%	7.6%	7.3%
18-21	23.0	15.2	16.3
22-24	20.5	13.7	14.6
Total 16-24	15.5	11.2	11.8

Source: U.S. Department of Commerce, Bureau of the Census, *Statistical Abstract of the United States: 1984* (Washington, D.C., 1983), table 254.

■ Many teenagers say they dropped out of high school because they did not like school. This is true for all white teens and for black males. The primary reason given by black females, however, is pregnancy; 40.4 percent of black female dropouts left school because they were pregnant.

TABLE 8.9

Self-Reported Major Reasons for Dropping Out of High School, by Sex and Race, 1978

| | Female | | Male | | |
Reason for Leaving School	Black	White	Black	White	Total
Received degree or completed coursework	2.8%	5.9%	3.8%	2.3%	3.9%
Marriage	4.2	17.1	1.0	2.3	8.2
Pregnancy	40.4	14.5	0.0	0.0	9.7
Other reasons; did not like school	14.7	23.3	28.9	37.4	27.5
Lack of ability; poor grades	4.6	5.5	8.1	8.5	6.3
Home responsibilities	9.7	5.9	4.2	3.2	5.4
Offered good work, chose to work	3.9	6.3	13.5	14.9	10.6
Financial difficulties; could not afford to attend	2.3	3.2	7.5	4.4	4.8
Entered the military	0.0	0.1	1.5	1.6	0.9
Expelled or suspended	4.8	1.1	13.5	10.4	6.2
School too dangerous	0.9	1.5	0.4	0.5	0.8
Moved away from school	0.0	3.6	2.1	2.2	2.8
Other	11.7	11.8	15.4	12.1	12.8

Source: U.S. Department of Labor, unpublished data from the Longitudinal Survey of Labor Force Behavior, Youth Survey, 1979.

Note: Data represent 18 to 21 year olds not enrolled in school who had completed fewer than 12 years of school.

Pregnancy and marriage are inextricably related among young white women dropouts, although marriage is far more commonly cited as the reason for leaving school. Whites cite marriage as a reason 4 times more often than do blacks; blacks give pregnancy as a reason 3 times more often than do whites.

Young black men drop out for financial reasons about 70 percent more often than young white men do. Young black women drop out because of home responsibilities more frequently than do young white women.

■ Young black and white high school graduates were equally likely to attend college in 1977. By 1982, whites were about 45 percent more likely to attend college.

TABLE 8.10

Percentage of Recent High School Graduates, 16 to 24 Years Old, Enrolled in College, by Year of High School Graduation and Race, 1977-1982

Year of Graduation	Black	White	Total
1977	50%	51%	51%
1978	46	50	50
1979	46	50	49
1980	43	50	49
1981	43	55	54
1982	36	52	51

Source: U.S. Department of Labor, Bureau of Labor Statistics, *Monthly Labor Review,* Vol. 106, No. 8 (Washington, D.C., August 1983), table 5.

■ Poverty significantly lowers young blacks' chances of attending college. Only 1 poor black high school graduate in 6 attends college. Among whites and blacks living above poverty, more than 1 high school graduate in 3 goes on to college.

TABLE 8.11

Educational Attainment Rates of 18 to 21 Year Olds, by Poverty Status and Race, March 1983

Family Income Level	Black	White	Total
Below poverty			
High school graduates	42.6%	52.8%	49.8%
1 year of college or more	8.0	16.2	13.6
1 year of college or more among high school graduates	18.8	30.7	27.3
Above poverty			
High school graduates	72.0	77.9	77.3
1 year of college or more	24.5	29.3	29.1
1 year of college or more among high school graduates	34.0	37.7	37.7
Total			
High school graduates	61.0	74.7	72.8
1 year of college or more	18.3	27.6	26.6
1 year of college or more among high school graduates	30.0	37.1	36.5

Source: U.S. Department of Commerce, Bureau of the Census, *Current Population Reports*, Series P-60, No. 144, "Characteristics of the Population Below the Poverty Level: 1982" (Washington, D.C., March 1984), table 13. Calculations by Children's Defense Fund.

More data on educational attainment of the adult population in appendix, table 26.

■ Almost 2 black children out of 5 are growing up in a family whose head did not complete high school, twice the rate for white children. White children, on the other hand, are almost 4 times more likely than black children to live in families headed by college graduates.

TABLE 8.12

Percentage of Children, by Family Type, Education of Family Head, and Race, March 1983

Family Type and Education of Family Head	Black	White	Total
Two-Parent			
Not high school graduate	34.2%	19.1%	20.4%
High school graduate	37.9	37.8	37.3
Some college	17.7	17.9	17.9
College graduate	10.3	25.2	24.5
Female-headed			
Not high school graduate	42.2	31.7	35.3
High school graduate	41.4	42.5	42.2
Some college	14.0	16.1	15.3
College graduate	2.4	9.7	7.2
Total			
Not high school graduate	38.0	20.9	23.2
High school graduate	39.9	38.4	38.2
Some college	15.9	17.7	17.5
College graduate	6.3	23.0	21.2

Source: U.S. Department of Commerce, Bureau of the Census, *Current Population Reports*, Series P-20, No. 388, "Household and Family Characteristics: March 1983" (Washington, D.C., May 1984), table 8. Calculations by Children's Defense Fund.

The educational gap between blacks and whites has narrowed some over the past 5 years. In 1978, white children were 4 times more likely than black children to live in families headed by college graduates.

9
LIVING CONDITIONS

Black children are more likely than white children to face harsh living conditions.

- Black teenagers are more likely than white teenagers to be victims of violent crimes. Black teenagers are also more likely to be arrested for violent crimes than are white teens.

- Black households are more than 3 times more likely than white households to occupy units that lack complete plumbing or are overcrowded or both. Fifteen percent of black households suffer from these conditions.

- Black households live without telephones or motor vehicles at 3 times the rate for white households. One-third of black households were without vehicles and 1 out of 10 lacked telephone service in 1980.

■ Black households are more than 3 times more likely than white households to occupy units that lack complete plumbing or are overcrowded or both. Fifteen percent of black households have these conditions.

TABLE 9.1

Percentage of Households Living in Housing Units with Incomplete Plumbing, Overcrowding, or Both, by Race of Householder, 1980

	Black	White	Total
Rented housing unit			
Incomplete plumbing	6.8%	2.9%	3.6%
Overcrowding	12.6	4.4	7.0
Both	1.5	0.3	0.6
Either or both	17.9	7.0	10.0
Owned housing unit			
Incomplete plumbing	3.9	1.1	1.4
Overcrowding	9.3	2.2	3.2
Both	0.7	0.1	0.2
Either or both	12.5	3.2	4.4
All housing units			
Incomplete plumbing	5.5	1.7	2.2
Overcrowding	11.2	2.9	4.5
Both	1.4	0.2	0.3
Either or both	15.3	4.4	6.4

Source: U.S. Department of Commerce, Bureau of the Census, *1980 Census of Housing, Vol. 1, Characteristics of Housing Units, General Housing Characteristics, United States Summary,* HC80-1-A1 (Washington, D.C., May 1983), tables 4, 11, and 12. Calculations by Children's Defense Fund.

Note: These are percentages of householders, not children. Overcrowding is defined as more than one person per room. Incomplete plumbing means that the housing unit lacks exclusive (not shared) access to hot and cold running water, a flush toilet, and a shower or bath.

Data on the percentage of children and female-headed families living in inadequate housing, 1976 and 1977, in appendix, tables 27 and 28.

■ Black households are 3 times more likely than white households to live without telephones or private means of transportation. They are more likely to rent housing than are white households, and more likely to live in less expensive housing.

TABLE 9.2

Percentage of Population Living in Housing with Selected Characteristics, by Race, 1980

	Black	White	Total
Living in owned housing unit	44.4%	67.8%	64.4%
Living in rented housing unit	55.6	32.2	35.6
Living in buildings with 5 or more units	26.7	15.4	17.2
Living with no telephone	16.1	5.5	7.1
Living with no vehicle	32.6	10.2	12.9
Median value of owned housing unit	$27,200	$48,600	$47,200

Source: U.S. Department of Commerce, Bureau of the Census, Statistical Abstract of the United States: 1984 (Washington, D.C., 1983), table 1342.

Note: Data are for householders, not children or families with children. These figures include adults living alone or with unrelated individuals, as well as families.

■ Black households are more likely than white households to live in neighborhoods inflicted with crime, trash, and abandoned buildings and to live with unsatisfactory police protection, health services, public elementary schools, and outdoor recreational facilities.

TABLE 9.3

Neighborhood Characteristics, by Race and Occupant Status, 1981

Characteristics	Owner Occupied		Renter Occupied	
	Black	Total	Black	Total
Neighborhood crime	24.3%	19.9%	33.0%	26.2%
Trash and litter	23.2	13.6	29.7	18.4
Boarded up or abandoned structures	16.6	6.1	23.6	10.8
Unsatisfactory police protection	13.6	9.6	17.5	11.2
Unsatisfactory outdoor recreation facilities	38.3	24.3	32.9	23.7
Unsatisfactory hospitals or health clinics	14.2	12.1	12.1	10.4
No grocery or drug store within one mile	13.8	20.6	8.3	9.6
No public transportation	33.4	49.0	18.7	28.7
Unsatisfactory public elementary schools	5.9	5.2	5.2	4.5

Source: U.S. Department of Commerce, Bureau of the Census, *Current Housing Reports,* series H-150-81, "Indicators of Housing and Neighborhood Quality by Financial Characteristics for the United States and Regions; 1981 Annual Housing Survey, Part B" (Washington, D.C., 1983), tables A-3 and A-7. Calculations by Children's Defense Fund.

■ Black teenagers are more likely than white teenagers to be victims of violent crimes; white teens are more likely than black teens to be victims of theft.

TABLE 9.4

Criminal Victimization Rates for Adolescents, by Race, 1982 (victims per 1,000 persons per year)

Age and Crime	Black	White	Total
12–15			
All personal crimes of violence	59.4	51.5	52.0
Rape	2.0	1.3	1.4
Robbery	21.3	8.3	10.2
Assault	36.1	42.0	40.5
All personal crimes of theft	115.4	131.7	127.4
16–19			
All personal crimes of violence	76.4	70.7	71.2
Rape	1.4	2.2	2.0
Robbery	25.0	9.4	11.9
Assault	49.9	59.2	57.3
All personal crimes of theft	106.7	131.5	127.9

Source: U.S. Department of Commerce, Bureau of the Census, unpublished data from the 1982 Criminal Victimization Survey.

■ Black youth make up about 15 percent of the youth population, but in 1983 they accounted for almost half the youth arrests for violent crimes and over one-fourth of the youth arrests for property crimes. Black youths accounted for over half the youth arrests for murder and aggravated assault and over two-thirds of the youth arrests for rape. Black adults accounted for under half the adult arrests for these crimes.

TABLE 9.5

Arrests for Violent and Property Crimes, by Race and Age, 1983

| | Under age 18 | | | Age 18 + | | |
| | | Percentage of Arrests | | | Percentage of Arrests | |
	Total	Black	White	Total	Black	White
Violent crime	74,604	48.8%	49.6%	368,096	46.0%	52.6%
Murder	1,345	57.4	41.5	16,682	49.6	49.0
Forcible rape	4,373	69.3	29.5	25,741	47.4	51.2
Robbery	35,195	39.4	59.4	98,673	60.1	38.7
Aggravated assault	33,691	54.7	44.0	227,000	39.4	59.1
Property crime	577,844	28.6	69.5	1,124,867	34.8	63.6
Burglary	158,842	26.5	72.1	255,762	34.5	64.4
Larcency-theft	376,152	29.9	68.1	789,493	34.9	63.3
Motor vehicle theft	36,403	26.9	70.9	68,892	35.1	63.3
Arson	6,447	15.9	82.8	10,720	27.7	71.1
Violent and property crimes	652,448	31.6	66.6	1,492,963	37.5	60.9

Source: U.S. Department of Justice, Federal Bureau of Investigation, *Uniform Crime Reports, Crimes in the United States, 1983*, (Washington, D.C., 1984), table 36.

Appendix

TABLE 1

Number and Projected Number of Children and Families in the United States, 1940-2000

Year	Children	Families	Persons Per Family	Children Per Family	Percentage of Families with Children
1940	45,656,000	31,491,000	3.76	1.24	—
1950	47,003,000	38,838,000	3.54	1.17	51.6%
1960	64,525,000	44,905,000	3.67	1.41	56.9
1970	69,762,000	51,456,000	3.58	1.31	55.9
1980	63,660,000	58,385,000	3.28	1.05	52.1
1984	62,140,000	61,997,000	3.24	0.99	—
Projections					
1990	64,337,000	68,458,000	3.01	0.93	—
2000	67,390,000	—	—	—	—

Sources: U.S. Department of Commerce, Bureau of the Census, *Current Population Reports*, Series P-60, No. 145, "Money Income and Poverty Status of Families and Persons in the United States: 1983 (Advance Data from the March 1984 Current Population Survey)" (Washington, D.C., August 1984), table 17; U.S. Department of Commerce, Bureau of the Census, *Current Population Reports*, Series P-20, No. 388, "Household and Family Characteristics: March 1983" (Washington, D.C., May 1984), table 1; U.S. Department of Commerce, Bureau of the Census, *Current Population Reports*, Series P-20, No. 391, "Households, Families, Marital Status, and Living Arrangements: March 1984 (Advance Report)" (Washington, D.C., August 1984), table 6; U.S. Department of Commerce, Bureau of the Census, *Current Population Reports*, Series P-25, No. 952, "Projections of the Population of the United States, by Age, Sex, and Race: 1983 to 2080" (Washington, D.C., May 1984), table 6; U.S. Department of Commerce, Bureau of the Census, *Current Population Reports*, Series P-25, No. 805, "Projections of the Number of Households and Families: 1979-1995" (Washington, D.C., May 1979), tables 1 and 3. Calculations by Children's Defense Fund.

Since 1940, the number of children in the United States has increased by 36.1 percent. The number of families has almost doubled over the same period.

TABLE 2

Marriages and Divorces, 1940-1983

Year	Marriages	Divorces
1940	1,596,000	264,000
1945	1,613,000	485,000
1950	1,667,000	385,000
1955	1,531,000	377,000
1960	1,523,000	393,000
1965	1,800,000	479,000
1970	2,159,000	708,000
1971	2,190,000	773,000
1972	2,282,000	845,000
1973	2,284,000	915,000
1974	2,230,000	977,000
1975	2,153,000	1,036,000
1976	2,155,000	1,083,000
1977	2,178,000	1,091,000
1978	2,282,000	1,130,000
1979	2,359,000	1,170,000
1980	2,413,000	1,182,000
1981	2,483,000	1,219,000
1982	2,495,000	1,180,000
1983	2,444,000	1,179,000

Sources: U.S. Department of Commerce, Bureau of the Census, *Statistical Abstract of the United States: 1984* (Washington, D.C., 1983), table 83; and U.S. Department of Health and Human Services, National Center for Health Statistics, *Monthly Vital Statistics Report,* Vol. 32, No. 12, "Births, Marriages, Divorces, and Deaths for 1983" (Washington, D.C., March 1984), p. 1.

The number of marriages in the United States reached almost 2.5 million in 1982, an historic high, before declining to 2.4 million in 1983. The number of divorces, however, rose at a much faster rate. In 1940, there was 1 divorce for every 6 marriages. In 1980, the ratio was 1 to 2. The number of divorces has remained fairly constant since 1980, averaging 1.18 million per year.

TABLE 3

Percentage of Children with an Absent Parent, by Cause and Race, 1970 and 1980

Year and Reason for Parent's Absence	Black	White	Total
1970			
Never married	4.6%	0.2%	0.8%
Separated	14.0	1.9	3.6
Divorced	4.5	3.4	3.6
Widowed	5.0	2.0	2.4
Other reason	3.3	1.2	1.5
Neither parent lives with child	8.6	1.2	2.3
Total with absent parents	40.0	9.9	14.2
1980			
Never married	13.2	1.1	2.9
Separated	15.6	3.5	5.3
Divorced	11.5	7.8	8.3
Widowed	4.4	1.9	2.3
Other	1.2	0.8	0.9
Neither parent lives with child	11.5	2.0	3.5
Total with absent parents	57.4	17.1	23.2

Sources: U.S. Department of Commerce, Bureau of the Census, *Current Population Reports*, Series P-20, No. 212, "Marital Status and Family Status: March 1970" (Washington, D.C., February 1971), tables 4 and 5; and U.S. Department of Commerce, Bureau of the Census, *Current Population Reports*, Series P-20, No. 365, "Marital Status and Living Arrangements: March 1980" (Washington, D.C., October 1981), tables 4 and 5. Calculations by Children's Defense Fund.

TABLE 4

Youths Incarcerated in Correctional Institutions, by Sex, Age, and Race, 1980

Age and Sex	Black	White	Total
Under 15			
Number	540	1,085	1,733
Rate per 1,000	0.1	0.0	0.0
15-19			
Male			
Number	17,730	23,734	45,669
Rate per 1,000	11.8	2.7	4.2
Female			
Number	782	1,367	2,363
Rate per 1,000	0.5	0.2	0.2
Total			
Number	18,512	25,101	48,032
Rate per 1,000	6.2	1.5	2.3
20-24			
Male			
Number	56,439	64,860	132,937
Rate per 1,000	44.0	7.4	12.5
Female			
Number	3,202	3,477	7,329
Rate per 1,000	2.2	0.4	0.7
Total			
Number	59,641	68,337	140,266
Rate per 1,000	22.0	3.9	6.6

Source: U.S. Department of Commerce, Bureau of the Census, *1980 Census of Population, Volume 1, Characteristics of the Population, Chapter D, Detailed Population Characteristics, Part 1, United States Summary*, PC80-1-D1-A (Washington, D.C., May 1984), table 266. Calculations by Children's Defense Fund.

Black youths, ages 15 to 19, are 4 times more likely than white youths to be placed in correctional institutions. Among youths, ages 20 to 24, blacks are more than 5 times as likely to be in such institutions.

TABLE 5

Residents of Juvenile Custody Facilities, by Race, December 31, 1979

Type of Facility	Black	White	Total
All facilities			
Public	13,752	26,053	43,234
Private	5,843	21,654	28,688
Short-term facilities			
Public	3,446	1,313	12,185
Private	106	547	733
Long-term facilities			
Public	10,306	18,740	31,049
Private	5,737	21,107	27,955

Source: U.S. Department of Justice, Bureau of Justice Statistics, *Sourcebook of Criminal Justice Statistics—1982* (Washington, D.C., 1983), tables 6.9 and 6.11.

TABLE 6

Estimated Pregnancy Rates,[a] by Pregnancy Outcome, Age of Women, and Race, 1980

Age of Woman	Nonwhite				White				Total			
	All Pregnancies	Live Births	Induced Abortions	Fetal Deaths	All Pregnancies	Live Births	Induced Abortions	Fetal Deaths	All Pregnancies	Live Births	Induced Abortions	Fetal Deaths
All ages	170.3	88.6	56.3	25.4	101.4	64.7	24.6	12.1	111.9	68.4	29.4	14.1
Under 15 years	9.8	3.9	4.7	1.2	1.8	0.6	1.1	0.2	3.2	1.1	1.7	0.4
15-19 years	181.3	94.6	64.9	21.8	95.8	44.7	38.3	12.8	110.0	53.0	42.7	14.3
20-24 years	266.0	145.0	94.9	26.0	168.1	109.5	43.4	15.2	183.6	115.1	51.6	16.9
25-29 years	211.6	115.5	64.7	31.4	157.3	112.4	24.8	20.0	165.7	112.9	31.0	21.8
30-34 years	148.2	70.8	38.5	38.8	85.9	60.4	13.6	11.9	95.0	61.9	17.2	15.8
35-39 years	68.1	27.9	20.4	19.7	31.2	18.5	7.6	5.2	36.4	19.8	9.4	7.2
40 years and older	18.8	6.8	7.4	4.6	7.5	3.6	2.9	1.0	9.1	4.1	3.5	1.5

Source: Stephanie J. Ventura, Selma Taffel, and William D. Mosher, "Estimates of Pregnancy Rates for the United States, 1976-81," Public Health Reports, Vol. 100, No. 1 (January-February 1985), table 2.

[a] Per 1000 women in specified age group.

TABLE 7

Births and Birth Rates, by Race, 1940-1983; and Projected Annual Births and Birth Rates, by Race, 1986-2000

Year	Black Number	Rate[a]	White Number	Rate[a]	Total Number	Rate[a]
1940	360,000[b]	26.7	2,199,000	18.6	2,559,000	19.4
1945	388,000[b]	26.5	2,471,000	19.7	2,858,000	20.4
1950	524,000[b]	33.3	3,108,000	23.0	3,632,000	24.1
1955	613,000[b]	34.5	3,485,000	23.8	4,097,000	25.0
1960	602,264	31.9	3,600,744	22.7	4,258,000	23.7
1965	581,126	27.7	3,123,860	18.3	3,760,000	19.4
1970	572,362	25.3	3,091,264	17.4	3,731,000	18.4
1971	564,960	24.4	2,919,746	16.1	3,556,000	17.2
1972	531,329	22.5	2,655,558	14.5	3,258,000	15.6
1973	512,597	21.4	2,551,030	13.8	3,137,000	14.9
1974	507,162	20.8	2,575,792	13.9	3,160,000	14.9
1975	511,581	20.7	2,551,996	13.6	3,144,000	14.8
1976	514,479	20.5	2,567,614	13.6	3,168,000	14.8
1977	544,221	21.4	2,691,070	14.1	3,327,000	15.4
1978	551,540	21.3	2,681,116	14.0	3,333,000	15.3
1979	577,855	22.0	2,808,420	14.5	3,473,000	15.8
1980	589,616	22.1	2,898,732	14.9	3,598,000	16.2
1981	587,797	21.6	2,908,669	14.8	3,646,000	15.9
1982	592,641	21.4	2,942,054	14.9	3,704,000	16.0
1983	—	—	—	—	3,614,000	15.5
1986	649,000	22.0	3,096,000	15.1	3,855,000	16.0
1987	653,000	21.8	3,107,000	15.1	3,873,000	15.9
1988	656,000	21.5	3,108,000	15.0	3,879,000	15.8
1989	656,000	21.2	3,097,000	14.8	3,871,000	15.6
1990	654,000	20.8	3,074,000	14.6	3,849,000	15.4
1995	629,000	18.7	2,868,000	13.2	3,628,000	14.0
2000	626,000	17.5	2,727,000	12.2	3,495,000	13.0

Sources: U.S. Department of Health and Human Services, National Center for Health Statistics, *Monthly Vital Statistics Report*, Vol. 33, No. 6, Supplement, "Advance Report of Final Natality Statistics, 1982" (Washington, D.C., September 28, 1984), Table 1; U.S. Department of Health and Human Services, National Center for Health Statistics, *Monthly Vital Statistics Report*, Vol. 32, No. 13, "Annual Summary of Births, Deaths, Marriages, and Divorces: United States, 1983" (Washington, D.C., September 21, 1984), p. 1; and U.S. Department of Commerce, Bureau of the Census, *Current Population Reports*, Series P-25, No. 952, "Projections of the Population of the United States by Age, Sex, and Race: 1982 to 2050" (Washington, D.C., May 1984), Table 2, Part B, Table 3, Part B, and Table 4, Part B.

[a]Births per 1,000 population.

[b]Data are for nonwhites.

There have been about 3.6 million births per year since 1980. The birth rates of blacks are consistently about 50 percent higher than those of whites. The annual birth rates for both blacks and whites are expected to decline through the year 2000. The total number of births each year will be about 3.8 million through 1990.

TABLE 8

Births to Adolescent Women, 1950-1982

Year	Number of Births	Births to Unmarried Adolescents	
		Number	Percentage of All Births to Adolescents
1950	425,000	59,200	13.9%
1955	490,000	72,800	14.9
1960	594,000	91,700	15.4
1965	599,000	129,200	21.6
1970	656,000	199,900	30.5
1971	640,000	203,600	31.8
1972	628,000	211,200	33.6
1973	617,000	215,800	35.0
1974	608,000	221,400	36.4
1975	595,000	233,500	39.2
1976	571,000	235,300	41.2
1977	571,000	249,800	43.7
1978	554,000	249,100	44.8
1979	560,000	262,700	46.9
1980	562,330	271,801	48.3
1981	537,024	269,828	49.9
1982	522,981	269,346	51.5

Sources: U.S. Department of Commerce, Bureau of the Census, *Statistical Abstract of the United States: 1984* (Washington, D.C., 1984), tables 85 and 97; U.S. Department of Health and Human Services, National Center for Health Statistics, *Monthly Vital Statistics Report*, Vol. 32, No. 9, Supplement, "Advance Report of Final Natality Statistics, 1981" (Washington, D.C., December 29, 1983), tables 2 and 15; and U.S. Department of Health and Human Services, National Center for Health Statistics, *Monthly Vital Statistics Report*, Vol. 33, No. 6, Supplement, "Advance Report of Final Natality Statistics, 1982" (Washington, D.C., September 28, 1984), tables 2 and 17. Calculations by Children's Defense Fund.

There were 523,000 births to adolescent women in 1982. The total number has declined since 1970 from a high of more than 650,000. The proportion of these births that are to unmarried women has steadily increased, however, and now stands at over 50 percent.

TABLE 9

Births to Unmarried Women, 1950-1982

Year	Number	Percentage of All Births	Percentage to Women under Age 20
1950	141,600	4.0%	41.8%
1955	183,300	4.5	39.7
1960	224,300	5.3	40.9
1965	291,200	7.7	44.4
1970	398,700	10.7	50.1
1971	401,400	11.3	50.7
1972	403,200	12.4	52.6
1973	407,300	13.0	53.0
1974	418,100	13.2	53.0
1975	447,900	14.2	52.1
1976	468,100	14.8	50.3
1977	515,700	15.5	48.4
1978	543,900	16.3	45.8
1979	597,800	17.1	43.9
1980	665,747	18.4	40.8
1981	686,605	18.9	39.0
1982	715,227	19.4	37.7

Sources: U.S. Department of Commerce, Bureau of the Census, Statistical Abstract of the United States: 1984 (Washington, D.C., 1984), table 97; U.S. Department of Health and Human Services, National Center for Health Statistics, Monthly Vital Statistics Report, Vol. 32, No. 9, Supplement, "Advance Report of Final Natality Statistics, 1981" (Washington, D.C., December 29, 1983), tables 15 and 16; and U.S. Department of Health and Human Services, National Center for Health Statistics, Monthly Vital Statistics Report, Vol. 33, No. 6, Supplement, "Advance Report of Final Natality Statistics, 1982" (Washington, D.C., September 28, 1984), tables 17 and 18. Calculations by Children's Defense Fund.

The number of births to unmarried women has risen for over 30 years, reaching over 700,000 in 1982. The proportion of these births that are to teenagers has been declining since the early 1970s, however, and reached 37.7 percent in 1982.

TABLE 10

Birth Rates for Unmarried Women, by Age and Race, 1970-1981 (live births per 1,000 unmarried women in specified age group)

Race and Year	15-19	20-24	25-29	Age of Mother 30-34	35-39	40-44	Total 15-44
Black							
1970	96.9	131.5	100.9	71.8	32.9	10.4	95.5
1971	98.6	130.6	99.6	68.6	32.7	10.1	96.1
1972	98.2	121.2	88.3	57.4	30.4	8.5	91.6
1973	94.9	116.0	84.5	57.8	27.6	7.7	88.6
1974	93.8	109.8	80.3	51.8	24.3	6.7	85.5
1975	93.5	108.0	75.7	50.0	20.5	7.2	84.2
1976	89.7	107.2	78.0	45.0	19.2	7.0	81.6
1977	90.9	110.1	78.6	45.7	19.0	6.6	82.6
1978	87.9	111.4	79.6	43.9	18.5	6.2	81.1
1979	91.0	114.1	80.0	44.8	19.3	5.9	83.0
1980	89.2	115.1	83.9	48.2	19.6	5.6	82.9
1981	86.8	112.5	86.4	47.2	20.4	5.8	81.4
1982	87.0	110.2	85.5	45.8	20.1	5.4	79.6
White							
1970	10.9	22.5	21.1	14.2	7.6	2.0	13.8
1971	10.3	18.7	18.5	13.2	7.2	1.9	12.5
1972	10.4	16.6	16.5	12.1	6.5	1.6	11.9
1973	10.6	15.5	15.9	10.6	5.9	1.7	11.8
1974	11.0	15.0	14.7	9.5	5.5	1.5	11.7
1975	12.0	15.5	14.8	9.8	5.4	1.5	12.4
1976	12.3	15.8	14.0	10.1	5.5	1.4	12.6
1977	13.4	17.4	14.4	9.3	4.9	1.4	13.5
1978	13.6	18.1	14.8	9.4	4.8	1.3	13.7
1979	14.6	20.3	15.9	10.0	5.1	1.4	14.9
1980	16.2	24.4	21.6	13.6	6.9	1.8	17.6
1981	17.1	24.9	20.7	13.6	6.8	1.8	18.2
1982	17.7	25.7	22.2	14.7	7.1	2.0	18.8

(continued next page)

TABLE 10 *(continued)*

Race and Year	15-19	20-24	25-29	Age of Mother 30-34	35-39	40-44	Total 15-44
Total							
1970	22.4	38.4	37.0	27.1	13.6	3.5	26.4
1971	22.3	35.5	34.5	25.2	13.3	3.5	25.5
1972	22.8	33.2	30.8	22.6	12.0	3.1	24.8
1973	22.7	31.5	29.6	20.3	10.8	3.0	24.3
1974	23.0	30.5	27.9	18.4	10.0	2.6	23.9
1975	23.9	31.2	27.5	17.9	9.1	2.6	24.5
1976	23.7	31.7	26.8	17.5	9.0	2.5	24.3
1977	25.1	34.0	27.7	16.9	8.4	2.4	25.6
1978	24.9	35.3	28.5	16.9	8.2	2.2	25.7
1979	26.4	37.7	29.9	17.7	8.4	2.3	27.2
1980	27.6	40.9	34.0	21.1	9.7	2.6	29.4
1981	28.2	40.9	34.7	20.8	9.8	2.6	29.6
1982	28.9	41.4	35.1	21.9	10.0	2.7	30.0

Source: U.S. Department of Health and Human Services, National Center for Health Statistics, *Monthly Vital Statistics Report*, Vol. 33, No. 6, Supplement, "Advance Report of Final Natality Statistics, 1982" (Washington, D.C., September 28, 1984), table 18.

The birth rate of unmarried black teens has declined since 1970, while the birth rate of white unmarried teens has increased. Among both black and white unmarried women in their twenties, the birth rates have been rising in recent years, although the rates of blacks declined from 1981 to 1982.

TABLE 11

Years of School Completed by Unmarried Mothers, by Race, 1981

| Years of School Completed | Black | | White | |
	Number of Women	Rate per 1,000 Women	Number of Women	Rate per 1,000 Women
Not a high school graduate	2,202,000	51.4	966,000	92.7
High school, 4 years	5,764,000	17.6	1,367,000	72.8
College, 1 year or more	5,984,000	5.8	968,000	34.0

Source: U.S. Department of Commerce, Bureau of the Census, *Current Population Reports*, Series P-20, No. 378, "Fertility of American Women: June 1981" (Washington, D.C., April 1983), table C.

Note: These are women of all ages, not only adolescent women.

TABLE 12

Median Family Income, by Race, 1970-1983 (1983 dollars)

Year	Black	White	Total	Black Income as Percentage of White Income
1970	$16,111	$26,263	$25,317	61.3%
1971	15,843	26,253	25,301	60.3
1972	16,347	27,504	26,473	59.4
1973	16,297	28,237	27,017	57.7
1974	16,175	27,088	26,066	59.7
1975	16,251	26,412	25,395	61.5
1976	16,175	27,192	26,179	59.5
1977	15,722	27,522	26,320	57.1
1978	16,614	28,050	26,938	59.2
1979	15,886	28,054	26,885	56.6
1980	15,324	26,484	25,418	57.9
1981	14,532	25,792	24,525	56.3
1982	14,035	25,394	24,187	55.3
1983	14,506	25,757	24,580	56.3

Source: U.S. Department of Commerce, Bureau of the Census, *Current Population Reports*, Series P-60, No. 145, "Money Income and Poverty Status of Families and Persons in the United States: 1983 (Advance Data From the March 1984 Current Population Survey)" (Washington, D.C., August 1984), table 3.

Median family income in real dollars was less in 1983 than it was in 1970. The relative decline in the income of black families is 5 times that of white families: 10.0 percent compared to 1.9 percent.

TABLE 13

Poverty Rates for Persons and Children, by Race, 1959-1983

| | | Persons | | | Children | |
Year	Black	White	Total	Black	White	Total
1959	58.1%	18.1%	22.4%	65.5%	20.6%	26.9%
1960	—	17.8	22.2	—	20.0	26.5
1961	—	17.4	21.9	—	18.7	25.2
1962	—	16.4	21.0	—	17.9	24.7
1963	—	15.3	19.5	—	16.5	22.8
1964	—	14.9	19.0	—	16.1	22.7
1965	—	13.3	17.3	—	14.4	20.7
1966	41.8	11.3	14.7	50.6	12.1	17.4
1967	39.3	11.0	14.2	47.4	11.3	16.3
1968	34.7	10.0	12.8	43.1	10.7	15.3
1969	32.2	9.5	12.1	39.6	9.7	13.8
1970	33.5	9.9	12.6	41.5	10.5	14.9
1971	32.5	9.9	12.5	40.7	10.9	15.1
1972	33.3	9.0	11.9	42.7	10.1	14.9
1973	31.4	8.4	11.1	40.6	9.7	14.2
1974	30.3	8.6	11.2	39.6	11.0	15.1
1975	31.3	9.7	12.3	41.4	12.5	16.8
1976	31.1	9.1	11.8	40.4	11.3	15.8
1977	31.3	8.9	11.6	41.6	11.4	16.0
1978	30.6	8.7	11.4	41.2	11.0	15.7
1979	31.0	9.0	11.7	40.8	11.4	16.0
1980	32.5	10.2	13.0	42.1	13.4	17.9
1981	34.2	11.1	14.0	44.9	14.7	19.5
1982	35.6	12.0	15.0	47.3	16.5	21.3
1983	35.7	12.1	15.2	46.3	16.9	21.7

Sources: U.S. Department of Commerce, Bureau of the Census, *Current Population Reports*, Series P-60, No. 76, "24 Million Americans: Poverty in the United States: 1969" (Washington, D.C., December 1970), table 1; U.S. Department of Commerce, Bureau of the Census, *Current Population Reports*, Series P-60, No. 145, "Money Income and Poverty Status of Families and Persons in the United States: 1983 (Advance Data From the March 1984 Current Population Survey)" (Washington, D.C., August 1984), tables 14 and 15; and U.S. Department of Labor, Employment and Training Administration, *Employment and Training Report of the President: 1982* (Washington, D.C., 1983), table G-9.

From 1959, when the first systematic national data on poverty were collected, to 1983, blacks have consistently been about 3 times more likely than whites to be poor. In 1959, 26.9 percent of all American children were poor. By 1969, this proportion had declined by about half, to 13.8 percent. Since 1979, the rate has risen dramatically to 21.7 percent. Similar patterns are observed for black and white children, although the absolute numbers are quite different. In 1983, almost half the black children were poor, compared to one-sixth of the white children.

TABLE 14

Children Living in Poverty, by Age and Race, 1983

	Black		White		Total	
Age	Number	Poverty Rate	Number	Poverty Rate	Number	Poverty Rate
Under 3	849,000	48.7%	1,747,000	20.0%	2,720,000	25.1%
3-5	797,000	50.3	1,655,000	19.7	2,582,000	24.9
6-13	1,819,000	46.2	3,692,000	17.1	5,780,000	21.9
14-15	463,000	44.1	870,000	14.6	1,399,000	19.3
16-17	456,000	42.9	814,000	13.7	1,326,000	18.3
Total under 18	4,384,000	46.7	8,778,000	17.3	13,807,000	22.2

Source: U.S. Department of Commerce, Bureau of the Census, *Current Population Reports*, Series P-60, No. 145, "Money Income and Poverty Status of Families and Persons in the United States: 1983 (Advance Data From the March 1984 Current Population Survey)" (Washington, D.C., August 1984), table 17.

Note: Includes children not in families.

Children are the poorest group in American society. More than 1 out of 5 were poor in 1983. More than half the children in female-headed families were poor, and over two-thirds of the black children in such families were poor. In general, the youngest children were the poorest.

TABLE 15

Persons and Families below the Poverty Level, by Race, 1983

	Black		White		Total	
	Number	Percentage	Number	Percentage	Number	Percentage
Persons						
All persons	9,885,000	35.7%	23,974,000	12.1%	35,266,000	15.2%
Children under age 18	4,258,000	46.3	8,456,000	16.9	13,326,000	21.7
Persons in families	8,381,000	34.7	18,269,000	10.7	27,804,000	13.8
Families						
All families	2,162,000	32.4	5,223,000	9.7	7,641,000	12.3
Husband-wife	533,000	15.5	3,135,000	6.9	3,820,000	7.6
Female-headed	1,545,000	53.8	1,920,000	28.3	3,557,000	36.0
Male-headed	84,000	23.7	168,000	10.4	264,000	13.0

Source: U.S. Department of Commerce, Bureau of the Census, *Current Population Reports*, Series P-60, No. 145, "Money Income and Poverty Status of Families and Persons in the United States: 1983 (Advance Data From the March 1984 Current Population Survey)" (Washington, D.C., August 1984), tables 14 and 15.

In 1983, 35.3 million people, or 15.2 percent of the population, lived in poverty. Over 21 percent of all children were poor. Almost half of all black children were poor, a rate almost 3 times that of white children. Over 7.6 million families were poor in 1983. Thirty-six percent of all female-headed families were poor, including almost 54 percent of black female-headed families. Female-headed families, regardless of race, are about 5 times more likely than husband-wife families to be poor. Black families in general are more than 3 times more likely than white families to be poor.

TABLE 16

Children, by Family Structure, Family Income, Labor Force Status of Mother, and Race, March 1984

Race, Family Structure, and Labor Force Status of Mother	Under $7,000	$ 7,000- $10,000	$10,000- $20,000	$20,000- $25,000	$25,000- $50,000	$50,000 +	Total
Black							
Husband-wife families	337,000	248,000	1,120,000	528,000	1,349,000	202,000	3,775,000
Mother in labor force	124,000	77,000	669,000	398,000	1,109,000	171,000	2,547,000
Mother not in labor force	213,000	171,000	450,000	121,000	241,000	31,000	1,228,000
Female-headed families	2,071,000	563,000	801,000	151,000	150,000	3,000	3,740,000
Mother in labor force	797,000	335,000	705,000	142,000	147,000	1,000	2,127,000
Mother not in labor force	1,276,000	228,000	95,000	9,000	3,000	1,000	1,613,000
Male-headed families	63,000	33,000	58,000	29,000	44,000	0	228,000
Total	2,473,000	844,000	1,979,000	699,000	1,544,000	205,000	7,743,000

Race, Family Structure, and Labor Force Status of Mother	Under $7,000	$ 7,000- $10,000	$10,000- $20,000	$20,000- $25,000	$25,000- $50,000	$50,000 +	Total
White							
Husband-wife families	1,972,000	1,549,000	8,374,000	5,306,000	17,887,000	5,552,000	40,641,000
Mother in labor force	623,000	534,000	3,888,000	2,900,000	10,862,000	3,597,000	22,403,000
Mother not in labor force	1,352,000	1,015,000	4,486,000	2,406,000	7,025,000	1,955,000	18,238,000
Female-headed families	2,661,000	911,000	2,123,000	514,000	584,000	76,000	6,869,000
Mother in labor force	1,094,000	603,000	1,879,000	471,000	544,000	54,000	4,644,000
Mother not in labor force	1,567,000	309,000	244,000	43,000	39,000	22,000	2,225,000
Male-headed families	151,000	57,000	256,000	118,000	322,000	59,000	962,000
Total	4,786,000	2,518,000	10,784,000	5,938,000	18,792,000	5,686,000	48,473,000

(continued next page)

TABLE 16 *(continued)*

Race, Family Structure, and Labor Force Status of Mother	Under $7,000	$ 7,000- $10,000	$10,000- $20,000	$20,000- $25,000	$25,000- $50,000	$50,000 +	Total
All Children							
Husband-wife families	2,426,000	1,949,000	9,851,000	5,943,000	19,806,000	6,016,000	45,991,000
Mother in labor force	783,000	633,000	4,713,000	3,357,000	12,350,000	3,949,000	25,786,000
Mother not in labor force	1,642,000	1,316,000	5,138,000	2,585,000	7,456,000	2,067,000	20,205,000
Female-headed families	4,846,000	1,542,000	2,980,000	676,000	756,000	79,000	10,878,000
Mother in labor force	1,916,000	986,000	2,623,000	621,000	712,000	56,000	6,914,000
Mother not in labor force	2,930,000	556,000	357,000	54,000	43,000	24,000	3,964,000
Male-headed families	221,000	100,000	321,000	147,000	376,000	62,000	1,226,000
Total	7,493,000	3,591,000	13,151,000	6,766,000	20,938,000	6,157,000	58,096,000

Source: U.S. Department of Labor, Bureau of Labor Statistics, unpublished data from the March 1984 Current Population Survey.

TABLE 17

Percentage of Children with Mothers in the Labor Force, by Age and Race, 1970-1984

Age and Year	Black	White	Total
Under 6			
1970	42.9%	26.3%	28.5%
1971	—	—	28.2
1972	42.6	27.1	29.1
1973	43.0	29.3	31.1
1974	45.1	31.1	32.9
1975	48.4	34.2	35.9
1976	49.8	34.6	36.5
1977	49.5	35.6	37.6
1978	52.0	38.5	10.5
1979	49.6	41.1	42.2
1980	51.4	41.7	43.0
1981	53.0	43.6	44.9
1982	52.9	44.8	45.8
1983	54.6	45.4	46.8
1984	55.0	47.3	48.2
6-17			
1970	52.1	44.8	43.2
1971	—	—	43.2
1972	49.7	42.9	43.8
1973	51.4	43.8	44.8
1974	51.9	44.9	45.9
1975	52.6	46.4	47.4
1976	53.9	48.6	49.3
1977	57.3	50.7	51.7
1978	60.7	52.3	53.6
1979	58.7	54.7	55.2
1980	59.8	56.5	57.0
1981	61.1	57.2	57.7
1982	60.8	58.7	59.1
1983	60.8	58.6	58.9
1984	63.0	60.0	60.3

(continued next page)

TABLE 17 *(continued)*

Age and Year	Black	White	Total
Total under 18			
1970	49.1	37.1	38.8
1971	—	—	38.8
1972	47.6	38.3	39.5
1973	48.9	39.5	40.7
1974	49.9	40.9	42.1
1975	51.4	42.8	44.0
1976	52.7	44.6	45.6
1977	55.2	46.4	47.7
1978	58.3	48.4	49.8
1979	56.2	50.7	51.4
1980	57.4	52.0	52.8
1981	58.7	52.9	54.5
1982	58.4	54.2	54.9
1983	58.8	54.2	54.9
1984	60.4	55.8	56.3

Sources: U.S. Department of Labor, Bureau of Labor Statistics, *Handbook of Labor Statistics* (Washington, D.C., December 1983), table 55; U.S. Department of Labor, Bureau of Labor Statistics, News Release USDL 84-321, "Number of Working Mothers Now at Record Levels" (Washington, D.C., July 26, 1984), tables 3 and 4; and U.S. Department of Labor, Bureau of Labor Statistics, unpublished data from the March Current Population Survey, various years. Calculations by Children's Defense Fund.

In 1970, black children, particularly preschoolers, were more likely to have working mothers than white children. Today, well over half of all children, black and white, have mothers in the labor force. Black children, regardless of age, are slightly more likely than white children to have working mothers. The differences between black and white children have lessened considerably since 1970, especially for preschool children.

TABLE 18

Labor Force Participation of Ever-Married Women with Children, 1947-1984

Year	Participation Rate
1947	18.6%
1948	20.2
1949	20.3
1950	21.6
1951	23.8
1952	23.8
1953	—
1954	25.6
1955	27.0
1956	27.5
1957	27.9
1958	29.5
1959	30.7
1960	30.4
1961	32.7
1962	32.9
1963	33.9
1964	34.5
1965	35.0
1966	35.8
1967	38.2
1968	39.4
1969	40.8
1970	42.0
1971	42.2
1972	42.9
1973	44.1
1974	45.7
1975	47.4
1976	48.8
1977	50.9
1978	53.0
1979	54.5
1980	56.7

(continued next page)

TABLE 17 *(continued)*

1981	58.3
1982	58.9
1983	59.5
1984	61.2

Sources: U.S. Department of Commerce, Bureau of the Census, *Current Population Reports*, Series P-50, Nos. 5, 11, 22, 29, 39, 62, 73, 81, and 87 (Washington, D.C., 1948, 1948, 1950, 1951, 1952, 1953, 1955, 1957, 1958, 1959); U.S. Department of Labor, Bureau of Labor Statistics, *Special Labor Force Reports*, Nos. 7, 13, 20, 26, 40, 50, 64, 80, 94, 120, 130, 144, 153, 164, 173, 183, 206, 216, 219, and 237 (Washington, D.C., 1960, 1961, 1962, 1963, 1964, 1965, 1966, 1967, 1968, 1970, 1971, 1972, 1973, 1974, 1975, 1977, 1978); U.S. Department of Labor, Bureau of Labor Statistics, News Release USDL 80-767, "Marital and Family Characteristics of Workers, March 1980" (Washington, D.C., December 9, 1980), table 4; U.S. Department of Commerce, Bureau of Labor Statistics, News Release USDL 81-522, "Half of Nation's Children Have Working Mothers" (Washington, D.C., November 15, 1981), table 2; U.S.Department of Labor, Bureau of Labor Statistics, News Release USDL 84-321, "Number of Working Mothers Now at Record Levels" (Washington, D.C., July 26, 1984), table 2; U.S. Department of Labor, Bureau of Labor Statistics, unpublished data from the March 1982 Current Population Survey and from the March 1983 Current Population Survey.

The labor force participation of ever-married mothers has increased more than three-fold since 1947, from 18.6 percent to 61.2 percent.

TABLE 19

Marital and Parental Status of the Labor Force, 1983

Family Relationship and Presence of Children	Number Employed	Percentage with Another Employed Person in Family
In families	82,644,000	73.4%
Husbands	37,505,000	62.4
With children under age 18	22,196,000	60.1
Wives	22,781,000	90.6
With children under age 18	12,231,000	94.6
Females who head families	4,686,000	34.8
With children under age 18	3,147,000	23.4
Males who head families	1,643,000	43.7
With children under age 18	666,000	30.7
Not in families	14,626,000	—
Total employed	97,270,000	—

Source: U.S. Department of Labor, Bureau of Labor Statistics, "Employment and Unemployment: A Report on 1983" (Washington, D.C., 1984, unpublished), table 53.

There are 3.4 million mothers in the labor force who are family heads. Two-thirds of these women have no other employed person in their family.

TABLE 20

Enrollment in Day Care Centers, by Age and Race of Children, 1977

Age and Race	Enrollment
Age	
Under 2	39,849
2	81,974
3	204,117
4	257,620
5	188,036
6	62,249
7-9	50,547
10+	13,341
Race	
Black	252,861
White	568,468
Total	897,733

Source: Craig Coelen, Frederic Glantz, and Daniel Calore, *Day Care Centers in the U.S.: A National Profile 1976-1977*, Final Report of the National Day Care Study, Vol. III (Cambridge, Mass.: Abt Associates, 1979), table 49.

Almost 900,000 children were enrolled in child care centers in 1977. About 30 percent of them, over 250,000, were black, even though black children make up about 15 percent of the population under age 18.

TABLE 21

Percentage of Persons without Health Insurance, by Type of Coverage of Other Family Members, Age, and Race, 1977

| Age and Race | Percentage of Coverage in Families of Uninsured Persons | | |
	Medicaid Only or With Other Insurance	Private Insurance or Other Excluding Medicaid and Medicare	No Insurance
All persons	5.9%	28.1%	43.2%
Children			
Under 6	6.2	28.2	57.7
6-17	5.7	27.3	54.6
Race, all persons			
White	4.4	28.6	44.7
Nonwhite	12.1	26.2	37.2

Source: U.S. Department of Health and Human Services, National Center for Health Services Research, *National Health Care Expenditures Study*, Data Preview 1, "Who Are the Uninsured?" (Washington, D.C., 1980), table 3.

Fifty-eight percent of uninsured children live in homes in which no other family member has insurance.

TABLE 22

Insurance Status of the Poor and Near Poor, by Age, Sex, and Race, 1977

Age, Sex, and Race	Number of Poor and Near Poor[a]	Always Medicaid	Insurance Status Sometimes Medicaid Otherwise Insured	Sometimes Medicaid Otherwise Uninsured	Always or Sometimes Privately Insured[b]	Always Uninsured
Age						
Under 18	12,600,000	31%	3%	14%	27%	34%
18-64	16,600,000	16	5	9	53	19
Sex						
Male	14,700,000	19	4	9	53	17
Female	20,400,000	23	5	10	49	12
Race						
White	26,400,000	17	4	8	58	14
Nonwhite	8,700,000	36	6	15	28	14

Source: U.S. Department of Health and Human Services, National Center for Health Services Research, unpublished data from the 1977 National Health Care Expenditures Survey.

[a]Poor and near poor includes those whose family income was less than or equal to the 1977 poverty level and those whose income was between 101 and 125 percent of that level.

[b]Includes individuals who had only Medicaid coverage.

TABLE 23

Percentage of Unemployed Persons Covered by Health Insurance, by Selected Characteristics, 1977

Characteristics	Number of Unemployed	Insured All Year	Never Insured	Lost Private Insurance	Other Part-Year Coverage
Unemployed at initial interview[a]	6,502,000	73.8%	11.1%	8.0%	7.1%
Age					
16-18	752,000	82.6	10.0	3.8	3.6
19-24	1,720,000	68.1	12.2	12.2	7.6
25-44	2,237,000	64.2	14.6	10.5	10.7
Race					
White	5,687,000	75.1	10.7	7.7	6.5
Nonwhite	815,000	64.8	13.8	9.9	11.6
Family income					
Poor or near poor	1,247,000	56.9	16.6	11.4	15.1
Low income	1,012,000	63.9	15.2	9.1	11.8
Middle income	2,528,000	75.4	11.0	8.7	4.9
High income	1,716,000	89.5	4.8	3.8	1.8
Employment status (last job)					
Full time	3,402,000	72.6	10.2	9.5	7.7
Part time	1,838,000	76.4	11.8	5.5	6.3
Occupation					
Professional, technical, managerial, administrative	850,000	77.7	5.2	10.4	6.7
Sales and clerical	1,329,000	76.2	9.1	9.0	5.7
Craftsmen, foremen, operatives	1,024,000	69.1	16.1	8.2	6.6
Service workers	1,414,000	76.8	10.4	6.4	6.4
Household composition					
No other worker	1,824,000	69.3	13.9	8.5	8.3
Uninsured working spouse or other worker	2,644,000	61.0	16.3	13.1	9.6
Insured working spouse	2,034,000	94.5	1.8	1.0	2.7

Source: U.S. Department of Health and Human Services, National Center for Health Services Research, unpublished data from the 1977 National Medical Care Expenditures Survey.

[a]Includes all other ethnic or racial groups not shown separately, persons with unknown health status, education, employment status, and occupation.

Lack of health insurance coverage is a serious problem among unemployed workers. Among the unemployed, the poor and near poor are less likely to be insured and more likely to lose insurance coverage. Unemployed craftsmen and service workers are almost twice as likely to be uninsured as are professional or clerical workers.

TABLE 24

Percentage of Black Public School Students Attending Majority Black Schools, by Racial Composition of School and School Year 1970-1976

| Racial Composition of School | Percentage by School Year | | | |
	1970-71	1972-73	1974-75	1976-77
99-100 percent black	24.17%	20.51%	19.48%	17.94%
90-99 percent black	16.57	15.15	14.31	13.97
50-89 percent black	25.24	26.41	27.02	28.14
Under 50 percent black	34.02	37.93	39.19	39.95

Source: U.S. Department of Education, Office for Civil Rights, "Distribution of Students by Racial/Ethnic Composition of Schools 1970-1976, Volume I: Users' Guide and National and Regional Summaries" (Washington, D.C., August 1978). Calculations by Children's Defense Fund.

Note: Data are for 1,910 school districts covering 88.5 percent of all enrolled black students (in 1976) for school years 1970-71, 1972-73, 1974-75, and 1976-77. "Black" in this table excludes children of Hispanic origin. Data collected since the 1976-77 school year are not comparable to previous data.

The proportion of black children in all-black schools declined during the 1970s. The proportion in primarily white schools increased during the same period.

TABLE 25

Percentage of High School Students Enrolled in Particular Courses, by Race and Sex, Fall 1979

Sex and Course	Black	White
Male		
Foreign language	13.6%	20.4%
Science	15.4	22.7
Mathematics	38.2	47.8
Took no academic or vocational course	21.0	13.6
Female		
Foreign language	17.0	29.9
Science	13.1	18.5
Mathematics	36.6	44.0
Took no academic or vocational course	15.3	11.6
All students		
Foreign language	15.3	25.1
Science	14.3	20.6
Mathematics	37.4	45.9
Took no academic or vocational course	18.2	12.6

Source: U.S. Department of Commerce, Bureau of the Census, unpublished data from the October 1979 Current Population Survey. Calculations by Children's Defense Fund.

White high school students are more likely than black high school students to be enrolled in foreign language, science, or mathematics courses. Black students, on the other hand, are about 50 percent more likely than white students to be enrolled in a career track course, whether academic or vocational.

TABLE 26

Years of School Completed by the Population 25 Years Old and Over, by Race, March 1982

Level	Black	White	Total
Elementary school			
Less than 5 years	7.3%	2.4%	3.0%
5-7 years	10.6	5.0	5.6
8 years	6.8	7.2	7.1
High school			
Less than 4 years	20.4	12.6	13.3
Graduate	32.5	38.8	37.9
College			
Some college	13.6	15.5	15.3
Graduate	8.8	18.5	17.7
Median Years of school	12.2	12.6	12.6

Source: U.S. Department of Commerce, Bureau of the Census, *Statistical Abstract of the United States: 1984* (Washington, D.C., 1983), table 223.

Black adults generally have lower levels of education than do white adults. They are three times more likely to have less than 5 years of elementary school and twice as likely to have only 5 to 7 years of schooling. They are also less than half as likely to be college graduates.

TABLE 27

Percentage of Children and Households with Children Living in Inadequate Housing, by Race, 1977

	Black	White	Total
All households with children	21.2%	8.9%	11.5%
Children	24.7	9.7	13.1

Source: U.S. Department of Housing and Urban Development, Office of Policy Development and Research, *Housing Our Families* (Washington, D.C., 1980), table 7.

Black children are more than twice as likely as white children to live in inadequate housing.

TABLE 28

Adequacy of Housing, by Type of Household, 1976

Type of Household	Percentage of Units With Flaws
All households	9.7%
Black households	21.4
Hispanic households	18.5
Female-headed households	12.0
Large households	16.9

Source: U.S. Department of Housing and Urban Development, Office of Policy Development and Research, *Housing Our Families* (Washington, D.C., 1980), table 2.

Over 1 out of 5 black households live in inadequate housing. One in 8 female-headed households lives in such housing.

TABLE 29

Children in America's 170 Largest Cities, 1980

City and State	Percentage of					Cities Ranked by[d]				
	Population under Age 18	Children Living in Poverty[a]	Teens[b] Not Enrolled in School or Graduated	Births to Teens[c] That Were Out of Wedlock	Children Not Living in Two-Parent Families	Population under Age 18	Children Living in Poverty[a]	Teens[b] Not Enrolled in School or Graduated	Births to Teens[c] That Were Out of Wedlock	Children Not Living in Two-Parent Families
Birmingham, Ala.	26.6%	31.3%	14.6%	74.2%	43.1%	91	17	86	40	28
Huntsville, Ala.	28.9	16.7	14.6	48.9	26.6	41	107	87	129	118
Mobile, Ala.	29.0	25.1	13.7	70.3	35.6	38	47	101	54	62
Montgomery, Ala.	30.2	27.0	14.4	72.5	35.7	19	39	90	45	61
Anchorage, Alaska	31.5	8.3	12.6	40.6	20.9	12	153	117	146	154
Mesa, Ariz.	30.1	9.3	11.9	45.0	17.0	20	147	125	139	166
Phoenix, Ariz.	29.0	13.7	21.9	56.1	24.8	37	132	13	107	132
Tempe, Ariz.	24.7	7.0	7.5	48.7	19.7	118	158	162	130	158
Tucson, Ariz.	25.5	16.7	13.7	49.0	27.0	105	108	102	128	112
Little Rock, Ark.	28.0	20.9	13.5	72.1	37.4	59	73	105	48	50
Anaheim, Calif.	26.5	10.2	15.9	40.3	23.7	94	143	62	147	140
Bakersfield, Calif.	29.1	15.5	17.7	53.3	27.6	35	118	47	115	109
Berkeley, Calif.	15.4	18.5	3.4	81.8	45.2	170	86	169	16	19
Concord, Calif.	27.8	7.0	10.5	43.6	23.5	69	157	141	140	142
Fremont, Calif.	30.1	5.5	10.7	50.9	18.4	21	165	139	125	161
Fresno, Calif.	27.9	23.0	17.2	63.4	32.8	60	59	50	81	83
Fullerton, Calif.	24.2	9.1	11.0	46.4	21.6	130	148	137	135	151
Garden Grove, Calif.	28.3	11.6	16.0	38.2	23.8	54	141	61	153	139
Glendale, Calif.	20.8	13.8	13.7	59.1	25.3	157	131	103	96	126
Huntington Beach, Calif.	27.9	7.6	9.6	41.3	21.2	61	155	149	144	152
Long Beach, Calif.	22.9	22.5	18.2	55.6	35.5	145	65	42	110	63
Los Angeles, Calif.	25.1	23.7	19.5	63.5	34.4	113	56	29	80	71
Modesto, Calif.	29.5	13.8	21.0	34.9	26.7	27	130	19	157	115
Oakland, Calif.	24.3	28.0	11.9	78.8	49.0	126	34	124	26	11
Oxnard, Calif.	33.2	17.1	25.4	37.7	26.4	6	101	4	154	120
Pasadena, Calif.	23.1	21.2	14.8	67.3	33.9	143	71	83	61	73
Riverside, Calif.	29.2	15.5	13.9	53.0	26.4	29	117	98	117	119
Sacramento, Calif.	24.6	22.3	15.1	61.0	35.7	119	66	75	91	59
San Bernardino, Calif.	28.1	24.4	22.0	61.5	37.7	57	51	11	88	49
San Diego, Calif.	24.1	16.6	11.8	51.4	28.7	131	109	127	123	103
San Francisco, Calif.	17.2	19.4	10.8	60.1	35.4	169	80	138	92	64
San Jose, Calif.	31.0	10.0	15.7	57.1	23.8	14	145	66	102	138

135

(continued next page)

TABLE 29 *(continued)*

Children in America's 170 Largest Cities, 1980

	Percentage of					Cities Ranked by[d]				
City and State	Population under Age 18	Children Living in Poverty[a]	Teens[b] Not Enrolled in School or Graduated	Births to Teens[c] That Were Out of Wedlock	Children Not Living in Two-Parent Families	Population under Age 18	Children Living in Poverty[a]	Teens[b] Not Enrolled in School or Graduated	Births to Teens[c] That Were Out of Wedlock	Children Not Living in Two-Parent Families
Santa Ana, Calif.	30.6	18.8	28.2	40.9	25.1	16	82	1	145	127
Stockton, Calif.	29.2	23.0	14.8	52.7	32.9	30	58	82	120	81
Sunnyvale, Calif.	23.0	5.8	12.4	40.3	22.9	144	164	120	147	147
Torrance, Calif.	23.8	5.2	7.8	47.3	20.1	134	167	159	133	157
Aurora, Colo.	29.5	6.9	14.7	39.6	20.7	26	159	85	150	156
Colorado Springs, Colo.	28.3	12.4	11.2	31.4	21.8	53	139	135	163	150
Denver, Colo.	22.5	20.2	21.0	64.7	34.8	147	76	18	76	67
Lakewood, Colo.	27.6	5.4	10.5	40.3	18.4	72	166	142	147	162
Pueblo, Colo.	28.5	19.0	12.7	51.4	25.7	48	81	116	123	123
Bridgeport, Conn.	27.9	34.0	22.3	72.8	46.6	63	8	7	43	14
Hartford, Conn.	29.0	39.3	20.8	85.1	55.9	40	2	20	6	4
New Haven, Conn.	25.3	35.3	14.9	85.3	49.5	109	6	77	5	9
Stamford, Conn.	24.5	12.6	9.3	71.5	24.9	124	136	152	51	130
Waterbury, Conn.	25.8	22.6	14.9	67.2	29.8	103	60	78	62	95
Washington, D.C.	22.5	27.0	12.7	88.1	58.4	146	40	115	2	2
Fort Lauderdale, Fla.	19.3	23.9	18.9	74.9	41.2	165	55	35	39	38
Hialeah, Fla.	24.2	15.7	14.9	29.7	24.7	129	115	80	166	133
Hollywood, Fla.	19.8	10.1	14.1	53.0	23.6	164	144	96	117	141
Jacksonville, Fla.	28.8	22.2	18.1	57.6	33.8	43	67	43	100	74
Miami, Fla.	21.4	34.1	20.4	71.7	43.8	156	7	22	50	24
Orlando, Fla.	24.0	27.2	17.6	23.6	45.6	133	38	48	120	16
St. Petersburg, Fla.	20.4	21.4	15.4	71.0	36.3	160	69	70	53	54
Tampa, Fla.	25.1	27.5	18.9	65.1	39.7	114	36	34	73	42
Atlanta, Ga.	26.8	39.2	15.5	83.3	56.5	86	3	68	13	3
Columbus, Ga.	29.5	24.5	16.9	51.9	36.0	25	50	53	121	56
Macon, Ga.	28.7	31.6	12.9	75.7	43.1	44	14	112	36	27
Savannah, Ga.	29.6	31.0	16.6	69.4	43.4	24	18	55	56	25
Honolulu, Hawaii	23.1	14.2	7.0	54.2	24.3	141	128	164	112	136
Boise, Idaho	26.8	9.6	11.8	43.4	22.3	89	146	128	141	148
Chicago, Ill.	28.4	30.8	20.1	81.8	44.0	49	20	25	16	23
Peoria, Ill.	27.6	18.0	13.0	83.4	29.2	71	88	110	12	99
Rockford, Ill.	27.8	14.1	21.6	66.5	25.5	68	129	14	68	124
Evansville, Ind.	24.6	17.6	16.9	54.3	28.5	121	94	54	111	104
Fort Wayne, Ind.	28.0	15.9	16.3	65.1	30.5	58	112	60	73	93
Gary, Ind.	34.9	28.5	13.8	84.9	46.4	2	30	99	7	15

136

TABLE 29 (continued)

Children in America's 170 Largest Cities, 1980

	Percentage of					Cities Ranked by[d]				
City and State	Popula-tion under Age 18	Children Living in Poverty[a]	Teens[b] Not Enrolled in School or Gradu-ated	Births to Teens[c] That Were Out of Wedlock	Children Not Living in Two-Parent Families	Popula-tion under Age 18	Children Living in Poverty[a]	Teens[b] Not Enrolled in School or Gradu-ated	Births to Teens[c] That Were Out of Wedlock	Children Not Living in Two-Parent Families
Indianapolis, Ind.	28.6	15.6	18.6	62.0	31.6	46	116	38	86	88
South Bend, Ind.	26.8	18.0	14.0	67.0	30.7	88	89	97	63	90
Cedar Rapids, Iowa	27.6	8.5	8.8	60.0	18.6	73	150	155	93	160
Davenport, Iowa	29.1	12.3	14.4	65.6	24.5	36	140	92	72	134
Des Moines, Iowa	25.9	14.3	14.6	56.1	26.1	100	125	88	107	122
Kansas City, Kans.	29.6	20.0	15.4	62.3	33.0	23	77	71	85	78
Topeka, Kans.	25.2	12.5	16.4	61.9	28.4	112	137	58	87	106
Wichita, Kans.	26.3	14.3	19.5	53.0	26.6	96	124	30	117	117
Lexington, Ky.	25.3	17.1	14.9	56.1	26.7	106	102	79	107	116
Louisville, Ky.	25.0	28.5	22.2	73.1	42.6	117	31	8	42	34
Baton Rouge, La.	27.3	24.6	12.0	61.1	36.6	78	49	122	89	53
New Orleans, La.	28.8	38.7	14.8	79.2	49.1	42	4	81	22	10
Shreveport, La.	30.3	23.5	15.5	71.9	36.9	18	57	69	49	52
Baltimore, Md.	26.9	32.5	20.3	88.5	54.0	85	11	24	1	5
Boston, Mass.	21.6	30.9	9.7	82.9	44.5	154	19	148	14	20
Springfield, Mass.	27.5	29.5	15.2	77.2	37.8	75	27	73	32	48
Worcester, Mass.	23.6	22.5	12.4	68.0	32.2	135	64	119	59	84
Ann Arbor, Mich.	19.1	8.5	2.9	51.9	25.0	166	152	170	121	129
Detroit, Mich.	30.3	31.5	21.2	79.4	51.9	17	15	17	20	7
Flint, Mich.	31.9	24.2	16.3	65.7	44.1	10	54	59	71	22
Grand Rapids, Mich.	27.4	18.4	13.8	61.1	33.1	77	87	100	89	76
Lansing, Mich.	29.2	17.2	14.4	63.3	34.1	31	100	91	82	72
Livonia, Mich.	28.4	2.1	4.7	58.5	10.3	52	170	168	97	169
Sterling Heights, Mich.	34.5	3.8	6.5	34.4	9.5	3	169	166	158	170
Warren, Mich.	27.8	6.4	9.0	43.4	16.4	67	162	153	141	167
Minneapolis, Minn.	20.0	18.0	15.6	75.8	35.7	163	91	67	35	60
St. Paul, Minn.	24.1	14.4	7.6	58.2	26.7	132	123	160	98	114
Jackson, Miss.	29.6	25.9	12.8	78.5	38.6	22	43	114	28	45
Independence, Mo.	27.2	7.6	17.8	38.3	18.2	80	156	46	152	163
Kansas City, Mo.	26.5	17.5	15.7	72.3	34.8	93	96	65	46	68
St. Louis, Mo.	26.1	33.7	22.0	35.4	52.3	98	9	10	156	6
Springfield, Mo.	23.2	16.2	10.0	84.2	23.3	139	110	146	9	143
Lincoln, Nebr.	23.5	8.5	7.0	53.8	19.6	136	151	165	113	159
Omaha, Nebr.	27.5	15.0	10.5	71.3	27.7	74	120	140	52	108
Las Vegas, Nev.	27.9	12.6	18.9	42.3	31.7	62	135	36	143	87
Reno, Nev.	20.1	6.8	19.6	33.9	28.9	162	160	27	159	101

TABLE 29 (continued)

Children in America's 170 Largest Cities, 1980

	Percentage of					Cities Ranked by[d]				
City and State	Population under Age 18	Children Living in Poverty[a]	Teens[b] Not Enrolled in School or Graduated	Births to Teens[c] That Were Out of Wedlock	Children Not Living in Two-Parent Families	Population under Age 18	Children Living in Poverty[a]	Teens[b] Not Enrolled in School or Graduated	Births to Teens[c] That Were Out of Wedlock	Children Not Living in Two-Parent Families
Elizabeth, N.J.	25.7	25.5	17.0	66.7	33.0	104	45	51	66	79
Jersey City, N.J.	29.4	33.3	19.5	82.7	45.4	28	10	28	15	17
Newark, N.J.	34.1	46.3	23.3	87.2	59.4	4	1	6	3	1
Paterson, N.J.	32.9	37.9	25.5	78.0	48.4	7	5	2	30	13
Albuquerque, N. Mex.	27.8	15.8	12.0	56.3	25.0	65	114	123	105	128
Albany, N.Y.	20.5	22.6	7.5	86.0	41.3	159	61	161	4	37
Buffalo, N.Y.	25.2	30.7	14.4	80.2	41.7	111	21	89	18	36
New York, N.Y.	25.0	31.8	15.8	79.0	40.5	115	12	63	24	41
Rochester, N.Y.	26.6	26.6	20.4	78.7	43.0	92	41	23	27	29
Syracuse, N.Y.	23.3	24.9	10.4	79.3	39.2	137	48	143	21	43
Yonkers, N.Y.	23.1	16.9	10.3	74.2	27.0	142	105	144	40	113
Charlotte, N.C.	27.8	17.3	14.7	76.0	33.6	66	98	84	34	75
Durham, N.C.	23.2	25.6	12.4	83.7	48.5	140	44	118	11	12
Greensboro, N.C.	25.3	17.3	8.6	66.5	32.9	107	99	156	68	82
Raleigh, N.C.	22.3	14.3	7.1	72.8	30.7	151	126	163	43	91
Winston-Salem, N.C.	25.3	22.5	9.5	76.3	41.9	108	63	150	33	35
Akron, Ohio	26.4	21.8	11.5	64.5	34.8	95	68	131	78	69
Cincinnati, Ohio	25.2	28.7	17.9	75.3	42.7	110	29	44	38	31
Cleveland, Ohio	27.8	31.3	18.4	77.8	43.3	64	16	39	31	26
Columbus, Ohio	25.8	21.3	14.1	66.3	34.7	101	70	95	70	70
Dayton, Ohio	27.4	29.7	16.4	75.4	42.8	76	26	56	37	30
Toledo, Ohio	28.1	18.8	13.0	67.0	29.1	56	83	109	63	100
Youngstown, Ohio	26.3	28.4	8.0	79.2	35.9	97	32	158	22	57
Oklahoma City, Okla.	27.0	15.5	17.6	46.7	28.4	84	119	49	134	105
Tulsa, Okla.	25.8	14.2	13.5	45.4	26.3	102	127	106	138	121
Eugene, Oreg.	22.4	11.5	8.2	59.8	24.9	149	142	157	94	131
Portland, Oreg.	21.8	16.1	16.4	64.6	31.0	153	111	57	77	89
Allentown, Pa.	22.4	18.7	9.5	62.4	27.6	150	84	151	84	110
Erie, Pa.	27.3	19.4	11.5	70.1	28.3	79	79	132	55	107
Philadelphia, Pa.	25.9	30.0	15.0	84.1	42.7	99	25	76	10	32
Pittsburgh, Pa.	21.4	24.3	9.8	80.2	38.0	155	53	147	18	47
Providence, R.I.	23.2	30.2	18.2	63.3	40.6	138	24	41	82	40
Columbia, S.C.	20.3	28.0	11.5	68.6	45.3	161	35	130	57	18
Chattanooga, Tenn.	26.7	25.4	13.6	65.0	38.3	90	46	104	75	46
Knoxville, Tenn.	21.9	26.4	11.6	48.3	35.1	152	42	129	131	65
Memphis, Tenn.	29.1	31.6	12.1	78.9	44.4	32	13	121	25	21
Nashville, Tenn.	25.0	17.6	15.2	56.2	33.0	116	93	74	106	80

TABLE 29 *(continued)*

Children in America's 170 Largest Cities, 1980

	Percentage of					Cities Ranked by[d]				
City and State	Population under Age 18	Children Living in Poverty[a]	Teens[b] Not Enrolled in School or Graduated	Births to Teens[c] That Were Out of Wedlock	Children Not Living in Two-Parent Families	Population under Age 18	Children Living in Poverty[a]	Teens[b] Not Enrolled in School or Graduated	Births to Teens[c] That Were Out of Wedlock	Children Not Living in Two-Parent Families
Amarillo, Tex.	29.0	12.4	19.7	28.6	20.7	39	138	26	167	155
Arlington, Tex.	28.5	5.1	14.4	24.4	16.1	47	168	93	168	168
Austin, Tex.	24.5	17.0	13.0	45.7	28.8	122	104	111	137	102
Beaumont, Tex.	28.3	20.4	10.2	57.6	29.4	55	74	145	100	97
Corpus Christi, Tex.	32.4	21.1	18.7	30.5	23.1	8	72	37	164	146
Dallas, Tex.	27.0	20.4	20.5	59.4	34.8	82	75	21	95	66
El Paso, Tex.	35.0	28.7	13.0	33.8	24.3	1	28	108	160	135
Fort Worth, Tex.	27.1	18.6	22.0	45.9	32.0	81	85	12	136	86
Garland, Tex.	33.7	6.1	19.0	35.5	17.2	5	163	33	155	165
Houston, Tex.	28.4	17.0	22.2	49.2	29.7	50	103	9	127	96
Irving, Tex.	29.1	6.4	21.4	30.3	21.1	34	161	15	165	153
Lubbock, Tex.	27.7	17.7	11.3	32.2	21.9	70	92	134	162	149
Pasadena, Tex.	31.4	8.8	25.5	23.8	18.2	13	149	3	169	164
San Antonio, Tex.	32.2	14.4	19.0	32.3	27.5	9	122	32	161	111
Waco, Tex.	24.3	27.4	11.8	50.2	36.1	127	37	126	126	55
Salt Lake City, Utah	24.2	18.0	21.3	39.2	24.0	128	90	16	151	137
Alexandria, Va.	18.3	15.9	15.4	68.5	35.9	167	113	72	58	58
Chesapeake, Va.	31.9	14.6	13.2	66.7	25.5	11	121	107	66	125
Hampton, Va.	29.1	16.8	8.9	53.3	30.6	33	106	154	115	92
Newport News, Va.	28.4	19.4	14.3	57.0	32.2	51	78	94	104	85
Norfolk, Va.	24.6	30.5	18.2	58.2	42.7	120	22	40	98	33
Portsmouth, Va.	28.7	28.3	19.4	72.2	40.9	45	33	31	47	39
Richmond, Va.	22.4	30.3	16.9	84.8	51.5	148	23	52	8	8
Roanoke, Va.	24.4	24.3	23.5	67.4	37.0	125	52	5	60	51
Virginia Beach, Va.	30.7	13.0	11.1	47.6	23.2	15	134	136	132	144
Seattle, Wash.	17.6	13.4	11.5	66.9	33.1	168	133	133	65	77
Spokane, Wash.	24.5	17.5	12.9	53.8	29.3	123	97	113	113	98
Tacoma, Wash.	26.8	17.5	15.8	57.1	30.1	87	95	64	102	94
Madison, Wis.	20.5	8.0	5.7	64.3	23.2	158	154	167	79	145
Milwaukee, Wis.	27.0	22.5	17.8	78.5	38.8	83	62	45	28	44

Source: 1980 Census data and National Center for Health Statistics 1982 natality data.

[a]Based on 1979 incomes.

[b]16 to 19 year olds.

[c]15 to 19 year olds.

[d]Ranks are based on the percentages of children affected by each of the categories.

Glossary

Age

Refers to age at last birthday.

Birth Rate:

The number of births in a calendar year per 1,000 persons as of July 1. An age-specific birth rate gives the number of births in a calendar year per 1,000 women of a given age.

Child:

A never-married person under age 18. One's "own child" can be a son, a daughter, a stepchild, or an adopted child.

Disability:

A physical, mental, or other health condition that has lasted 6 months or longer and limits or prevents a particular type of activity, such as working at a job or business.

Ever Married:

Describes a person currently married or separated, as well as those widowed or divorced.

Family:

Two or more persons who are related by birth, marriage, or adoption and who live together as a household. See Household.

Family Type or Structure:

Families are classified according to the sex of the householder and presence of relatives. See Householder.

- **Married-Couple Family:** Householder and spouse are members of the same household. Also called a two-parent family (if children are present) or a husband-wife family.

- **Female-Headed Family:** Householder is a female and her husband is not present in the household.

- **Male-Headed Family:** Householder is a male and his wife is not present in the household.

- **One-Parent Family:** Householder, with children, is either a male or a female with no spouse present in the household. Also called a single-parent family.

Group Quarters:

Non-household living arrangements that include 5 or more persons unrelated to one another. Group quarters are of two types: institutions and other. Institutions include homes for the aged, mental hospitals, correctional facilities, etc. Other group quarters include rooming and boarding houses, military barracks, college dormitories, etc.

Household:

Person or persons occupying the same housing unit. Households are classified by the sex of the householder and presence of relatives, i.e., family or nonfamily. Also see Housing Unit.

Householder:

The person designated as the reference person for the household. This person is one of the persons in whose name the housing unit is owned or rented. If there is no such person, the householder is an adult at least 15 years old who is not a roomer, a boarder, or a paid employee.

140

Housing Unit:

A house, apartment, mobile home, or trailer, group of rooms, or single room occupied as a separate living quarter by a household. Separate living quarters are those in which the occupants live and eat separately from any other persons in the building and which have direct access from the outside of the building or through a common hall.

Income:

Total money received for a specific calendar year by persons age 15 or older. Income is received from wages and salaries, farm and non-farm self-employment, interest, dividends, net rentals, Social Security, public assistance, and other. Income is the amount of money received before deductions for personal income taxes, Social Security or Medicare payments, union dues, etc. Also see Per Capita Income.

- **Family Income:** Total income received in a calendar year by all family members age 15 or older.

- **Household Income:** Total income received in a calendar year by all household members age 15 and older.

Infant:

A child under one year of age.

Infant Death Rate:

The number of infant deaths (deaths of children under one year of age) in a calendar year per 1,000 children under age one as of July 1.

Infant Mortality Rate:

The number of infant deaths (deaths of children under one year of age) in a calendar year per 1,000 live births in that same year.

Labor Force:

The total number of persons age 16 or older who are either employed or looking for work. The labor force includes members of the armed forces. A person is not in the labor force if he or she is age 16 or older and neither employed nor looking for work; for example, students, homemakers, retired persons, inmates of institutions, and persons doing unpaid family work.

Median:

Describes the point which divides a population into two *equal* groups. For example, median income divides people, families, or households by those who have income less than the median and those who have incomes greater than the median.

Per Capita Income:

The total income for a group divided by the number of individuals in that group. It is the average amount of income received by each person in the group.

Poverty Level:

The amount of income, as determined by the federal Office of Management and Budget, below which a family or individual is considered poor. The poverty level varies by the size of the family or household. It is adjusted every year to account for inflation. The poverty level for 1982 was $10,200 for a family of four.

Poverty Rate:

The percentage of the population that is below the poverty level. Poverty rates are calculated for persons and for families.

Prenatal Care:

Medical care during pregnancy. Early prenatal care is that begun during the first three months (first trimester) of pregnancy. Late prenatal care is that begun during the last three months of pregnancy.

Race:

Persons related by common descent. The Census Bureau and other government agencies usually use 5 race categories: white; black; American Indian, Eskimo, and Aleut; Asian and Pacific Islander; and other. Note that Hispanic or Spanish origin is not a category of race.

Rural Area:

Any place of fewer than 2,500 population.

Single:

Describes persons who have never been married, including persons whose only marriage was annulled.

Unemployment Rate:

The percentage of the civilian labor force that is unemployed.

Urban Area:

Any place of 2,500 or more population.